Praise for *WORKING ON YOURSELF DOESN'T WORK,*
A Book About Instantaneous Transformation® – Ariel & Shya Kane

"#1 Best Book Buy. 10+ RATING! A 'must' for the library of every seeker of truth!"

-Awareness Magazine

"#1 Best Seller in Self-Help/Personal Transformation & Satisfaction categories."

-Amazon.com

"Don't let the title mislead you. *WORKING ON YOURSELF DOESN'T WORK* is not about the futility of self-improvement, but rather about the effortlessness of transformation... A simple, easy-to-read book with a valuable message that can take you through the swamp of the mind into the clarity and brilliance of the moment."

-Whole Life Times

"I strongly recommend this book! Ariel & Shya Kane are highly skilled, experienced guides who point the way to the clarity of the present moment. They are at the forefront in the field of personal transformation and have much to offer anyone who wants a more meaningful and fulfilling life."

-Paul English, Publisher, *New York Spirit Magazine*

"A great book which I so enjoyed reading!... It inspired me to re-examine my life and my personal beliefs so that I now function on a much higher level."

-Magical Blend Magazine

"This warm, accessible book will illuminate and befriend your transformation."

-Personal Transformation Magazine

"This book is a must read. One to have on your bookshelf, to share with your friends."

-To Your Health Magazine

"Ariel and Shya Kane actually "walk the talk"... This simple, yet profound book teaches us how to live in the moment. *WORKING ON YOURSELF DOESN'T WORK* is refreshing, truthful, sincere, authentic and written with insightfulness and clarity."

-Dr. Maryel McKinley

$12.95 Paperback – ISBN: 1-888043-04-0
$19.95 CD – ISBN: 1-888043-11-3
$14.95 Downloadable Audiobook available at: www.ask-inc.com

Praise for *HOW TO CREATE A MAGICAL RELATIONSHIP* –
Ariel & Shya Kane

"Years of therapy cannot touch what the Kanes can do in minutes...
10 stars for this outstanding work."
- Dr. Maryel McKinley, *Awareness Magazine*

"A masterpiece... unprecedented by any other relationship genre book
this reviewer has ever come across."
- *Wisdom Magazine*

"A fresh new approach to age old problems."
- *New York Spirit*

"Excellent... a strong guide for those looking for direction in their
relationships."
- *Foreword Magazine*

"... you need to read this most incredible book that just might change
the way you look at yourself, your partner, and yes - your relationship."
- Inner Tapestry, *Maine's Holistic Journal*

"The Kanes are really on to something. The book reads easily, not
dancing around serious issues, and not getting bogged down in self-help
vernacular."
- *New York Resident Magazine*

"Ariel and Shya Kane's book will help you create vital, supportive
partnerships that flow smoothly day in and day out, not just when
things are easy."
- *Nexus Magazine*

"This is a well-written book with lots of positive self-affirming directions
and is the first of the self-help books about living in the moment that
effectively tackles the problem of relationships. This is a highly recom-
mended book."
- Harold McFarland,
Readers Preference Reviews & Midwest Book Review

"In this book, you will learn the key elements that transform an
ordinary and mundane relationship into a miraculous one."
- Hispano News

$16.95 Paperback – ISBN 10: 1-888043-14-8, ISBN 13: 978-1-888043-14-3
$14.95 Downloadable Audiobook available at: www.ask-inc.com

What People Are Saying About *BEING HERE* – Ariel & Shya Kane

"I've had a lot of experience with 'doing' things to achieve a sense of well being in my life. Little did I know that simply 'Being Here' was all I needed!"

- Roderick Hill, Actor

"The Kanes produce pure magic! *Being Here* is a must-read if you want the true secrets to living a magnificent life."

- Marie Forleo, Author of *Make Every Man Want You*

"These entertaining stories have touched my life in profound ways, leading me to the moment time and time again."

- Paula Serios, Marketing Executive

"So gently told, yet the impact is profound – this book is a gift to anyone who wants a magical life."

- Elizabeth Ward, Costume Designer

"If you want to laugh, cry, feel your own compassion and humanity – don't miss Being Here."

- Johnnie M. Jackson, Jr., Attorney

"When I find myself upset, one of Ariel & Shya's stories will pop into my head and instantaneously I am feeling well in myself. Never underestimate the power of a great story. This book is full of them."

- Colleen Campbell, Loan Administrator

"*Being Here* is compassionate, entertaining and inspiring... a practical guide to living the life of your dreams."

- Valerie Paik, Website Developer

"*Being Here* can Transform your life. Just let your emotions swirl and light a fire under your aliveness as you read about everyday folks that the Kanes have coached and whose lives are now magnificent!"

- Joe Cilmi, Yoga Instructor

Being Here

Modern Day Tales of Enlightenment

ARIEL & SHYA KANE

ASK PRODUCTIONS, INC.

Edited by – Andrea Cagan
Cover and Layout Design – Fernanda Franco
Kanes' Photos – William B. Sayler
Butterfly Cover Photo – William B. Sayler

Library of Congress Catalogue Card Number: 2007923432

Kane, Ariel.
  Being here : modern day tales of enlightenment /
Ariel & Shya Kane.
    p. cm.
    ISBN-13: 978-1-888043-18-1
    ISBN-10: 1-888043-18-0

    1. Self-actualization (Psychology)   I. Kane, Shya.
II. Title.

BF637.S4K36 2007   158.1
                              QBI07-600034

Printed in the United States of America.

For information contact:
ASK Productions, Inc.
457 Route 579
Milford, NJ 08848-2131
        or
website: www.ask-inc.com
email: kanes@ask-inc.com

Instantaneous Transformation® is a registered trademark of ASK Productions, Inc.

Authors' note: many of the names in these stories have been changed to preserve privacy.

For all those who enter upon the journey of Self-Discovery
and have the courage to keep going.

And

For those who look beyond the intention of "fixing" themselves
to discover the magic in being of service, as that is what
Self-Discovery is ultimately about.

Table of Contents

ONE DAY, after taking every self-help workshop available, being an EST trainer candidate and seminar leader, living for years in a meditation center, Shya Kane stopped trying to improve himself.

In that moment, 20 years ago, he became enlightened.
He immediately stopped trying to fix or change his wife Ariel.
Soon – she became enlightened. Their lives shifted into an effortless, joyous adventure.

As they interact with their world, magical events take place...

PREFACE

In recent years, many people have seen the value of meditation and other disciplines. However, carving time out for yourself each day is not the only way to access well-being and enlightenment.

Over the years, the two of us have discovered the majesty, magic and transformational properties of simply *Being Here*. Where each interaction, each moment is filled with juice and life and all the components necessary to have your life transform. Where living your life to the fullest in each moment without judging yourself becomes the greatest game and the most natural meditation of them all.

As children, our imaginations were ignited by stories. As we have grown, the two of us have seen the power that a good tale has to inspire, amuse, entertain and yes, even enlighten.

When you get involved in another's story, you often forget the story of your own life. If you forget it long enough, it might just leave you alone and the limitations contained in your personal script can fall away. We have seen over and over how when people get engaged in *Being Here*, in this moment, old limiting ideas simply cease to hold sway.

Before each section of this book we have included a short introduction, a guide of sorts, that will support you in savoring the limitless possibilities waiting for your discovery.

We invite you to take a journey into *Being Here*. That is enough to simply, easily have a reality shift where you suddenly find yourself lighter, freer and more alive. *Being Here* is all it takes to have Instantaneous Transformation. Join us as we take you with us into distinct moments in our lives and the lives of our friends and family as we discover the richness and majesty of being alive. Being in the moment can transform even an ordinary circumstance into a profoundly moving, enlightening event.

Run breathlessly with us down the streets of Hell's Kitchen in Manhattan. Gaze out of our picture window into our backyard. Save yourself from the undertow at the beach and dream with us in Bali.

We hope you enjoy the journey. We did. We still are...

Warmly,
Ariel and Shya Kane

FORGIVENESS AND COMPASSION

Most of us do not realize that when we forgive someone, we are actually freeing ourselves. When we forgive, we extricate ourselves from the entanglement of a disturbing situation or circumstance.

Compassion allows us to walk a mile in another person's shoes, to avoid judging another or ourselves for actions over which we had little or no control.

These three stories will support you in discovering new possibilities while navigating the uncharted waters of your own life. Perhaps you will even find that elusive state of grace that comes when you really, truly find forgiveness and compassion for all that it means to be human.

ABOUT COMPASSION
As told by Ariel

When I casually glanced over my shoulder, the man was sprinting after me, murder in his eyes...

The year was 1982 and I was 24, an actress, living in Hell's Kitchen, a midtown area on Manhattan's west side. There, I rented a small one bedroom apartment on the second floor of a building between 9th and 10th Avenues, not a particularly safe neighborhood. One morning I came out of my building, groggy, on my way to work, when I literally ran into yellow crime scene tape protecting an area on the sidewalk across from my apartment. A man had been stabbed to death. I knew the area was dangerous but I had gotten cocky.

One lovely Wednesday afternoon near dusk I was preparing to leave my building on my way downtown when I was greeted by a pungent odor. The entrance to the four-story walkup had two sets of doors; the outer one to keep the weather out, and the inner locked one to keep intruders out. On and off during the past month or so, a vagrant had taken to sleeping between the inner and outer set of doors and sitting for hours on the stoop. He was at least six-feet tall, large and unwashed, and I always had to quash my fear as I stepped over or around him. The police had been called a few times and herded him away from my doorstep but he always seemed to return as if drawn by a magnet.

Earlier in the week as I left the building, I trailed another woman on the stairs who was on her way out. As she reached the front doors, I noticed that our resident street person had once again draped himself across the entryway. I don't know if this was her normal style, or if she was emboldened because there were now two of us, but she quickly whipped open the door and shouted, "Out! Get out! You don't belong here! That's right. Sit up. Move it! You aren't supposed to be here. Get out!"

Like molasses on a cold day he slowly sat, then stood. He stepped outside and as my neighbor stood glowering, he shuffled down the stairs and moved off down the street, perhaps to haunt another doorway. Filled with indignation the woman watched until he was well on his way, then she turned the opposite direction and stomped off, still in a huff.

On this particular evening, when I saw that he was back, I paused on the step, frozen in indecision. Should I return to my apartment and call the police again? If I did that I would be late for an appointment. Should I open the door and simply step over him like I had in the past? This option made my skin crawl. I had done it, but I hadn't liked it. Then I thought of my neighbor's tactic for making the man move.

Well, why, not? I thought. Mentally I fortified myself, *It's my entrance, not his.* The more I thought about it, the more justified I felt. *I pay rent here – he does not.*

Soon I was ready to battle the demon at my door, slay the dragon, fight for my rights as a tenant. Before you could say, "Whoa, wait a minute, here," I was filled with the righteousness of someone young and foolish, one who had never been subjected to truly devastating events in her own life. Sure, I had lost people I had loved, broken up with boyfriends, given a rotten audition or two, been homesick, been ill and yet, even though I had lived in New York

City for years on my own, I was still immature and naive, untouched by true misery.

As I reached the front door, I stood tall and tried to look tough, a caricature of someone older, wiser and in charge. Swinging the door open I yelled in my best rendition of what I had seen my neighbor do. "Get up and get out! Move it. This isn't a place to sleep!"

I continued to rant as he hoisted himself up from his cold, hard bed between the doors and made his way out to my stoop. But it wasn't enough. I wanted him gone.

"Now, keep going! You know you aren't supposed to be here. It is private property. Move down the street."

And so he moved – slowly, gingerly. When I think of it now, I am reminded of crocodiles that I have watched from the safety of a bridge over a river in Costa Rica. You know in your heart that they are dangerous but they seem so placid in the sun. The really large crocs, 20 feet long or more, draw your eye and you want to stare and prod them to action just to see what they will do. Although they can be deceptively still, the power in their massive bodies is unleashed when given cause to move. A frenzy of activity, frothy and violent, erupts when a chicken carcass is dropped their way.

Satisfied that I had moved the street person from my doorstep and into the street where he belonged, I sauntered down the sidewalk, heading for the bus stop. A few moments later, when I casually glanced over my shoulder, the man was sprinting after me. In a burst of adrenaline I ran. My high heels weren't made for running, but I did it anyway. In a panic, I rounded the corner of 10th avenue and dashed into a little bodega where I knew the owner, a large Polish man who had been polite to me over the years. Hastily, I scurried to the back of his narrow store and darted behind him, just as the enraged vagrant slid into view and stood quivering at the entrance to the store. He lifted his big paw and pointed a finger right at me: "You, you, I'll get you!"

I was shaking. I knew that if I had not found cover I would have been in serious trouble, beaten or dead. It had yet to set in that I still had to go home that night and face the man, if he was still there. I was safe for the moment.

The Polish storeowner, Mr. Nijinsky, clearly wasn't pleased. "You can't run in here to get away from trouble. I don't want trouble on my doorstep."

After a bit of breathing space, when I got my trembling under control, I apologized to Mr. Nijinsky and promised it would never happen again. Privately, I wished he had been more sympathetic. He could have at least called the police or something. Hesitantly, I went to the doorway and looked down the street in both directions and saw that the coast was clear.

I was too shaken to take a bus. I hailed a taxi and rode downtown to meet Shya, whom I was dating at the time, and to do some volunteer work, which had been my evening plans before I had been so rudely and almost violently interrupted. When I sat next to Shya's desk at work, I began to cry. My breath came in gulps, my eyes spurting hot tears as I gasped out my story. Shya took my hand, sat back in his chair and became very still.

I began to relax, my sobs quieted and I became calmer. Yet my mind kept flicking back to thoughts of what might have been had I not glanced back, of what would have happened if the man had caught up to me. Images of him flashed, framed by the store's doorway, quivering and barely able to control his rage.

Shya leaned forward, looking intently at me. "Ariel, we have to go back there and you have to apologize to that man. You forgot. He's a human being and you just treated him like dirt."

This was certainly not what I had expected to hear. I expected sympathy, outrage, and fear on my behalf. But in an instant I, too, became still. Shya was right. I could feel it in my heart. I could feel it in my skin and muscles and my shoulders as they dropped. As I sat there, I realized it had been a mistake to emulate my neighbor. Just because I had seen another person act that way did not make it the right thing to do, and it certainly didn't make it true for me. I started to remember things about the vagrants I had seen in Portland, Oregon when I was a child. Their desolation had touched me so much that in my childhood innocence I often had daydreams of bringing them home with us and making them feel better. My sisters and I had frequently remembered them in our prayers. I began to cry again as I found myself wondering what had happened to my innocence. Shya sat back and let me weep.

I did my volunteer work that evening but my mind kept roving between what had just happened and what was to be. I kept bringing my scattered thoughts back to what I was doing but it was a challenge. Soon it was 11pm and time to go home.

This was when Shya still rode his motorcycle, a blue Yamaha 650 Special affectionately called, "Old Blue." We got on and rode back to Hell's Kitchen to meet the devil that had been in front of my door. Truthfully the devil was my pride and it was time I swallowed some, but I didn't know if the man would be there. If he were, what I would say?

We cruised down West 49th street to my home, number 454, a brownstone on the left side. The man was not on my steps, nor in front of my entryway. He had moved one doorway further down to a vacant building. There he lay, at the top of the steps, reeking and still, but I knew the potential for danger was simply slumbering and could awake in an instant. Shya slowly glided the bike past my building and coasted to a stop at the bottom of the steps where the vagrant slept. As we approached, the fellow eased himself into a sitting position and glared down at me from above. I swung my leg over, stepped off the bike and approached alone.

I could tell the man was preparing for more abuse. His shoulders hunched. He gripped the step.

"Sir," I said in a quavering voice. "I am here to apologize. I spoke badly to you today and it was wrong of me. I'm sorry."

Now, suddenly, I realized what I needed to let this individual know. "You see, the truth is, I'm afraid of you. You are a lot bigger than me and when I come down the steps and you are on my stoop or in front of the doors I get scared. I just tried to get you to move because I was afraid. But I was mean. I hope you will forgive me because it wasn't right. I am really, truly sorry."

I stood looking up and he sat there looking down. But I knew that I had spoken to him, person-to-person, equal-to-equal, admitting my fear and asking for his compassion for my situation. And in so doing I found my compassion for his situation, too.

I never spoke with him again. But then, he never sat in front of my door again either. I was careful coming and going from my home for a while, but on those days when he was sitting on the steps next door he was not moved to bother me. I would cautiously nod my head in passing as I went about my day.

I later learned that the man's name was Mr. Fitzgerald. He had once owned the brownstone across the street from my apartment before he fell on hard times. This was before, as street legend had it, his wife had died tragically at a young age from some condition that no one in the neighborhood seemed to remember.

He *was* drawn to my doorstep as if by a magnet. He used to stare at the home where his beloved wife had died. I don't know what ever became of Mr. Fitzgerald. He drifted away in time and I went on with my life. But I do know that he taught a foolish young woman a simple yet poignant lesson about compassion.

SEE DICK TRANSFORM
As told by Shya

At 15, I got my first boat. Well, that was the fantasy. I didn't actually own a boat but I bought a used ten-horse power Evinrude outboard motor and I would rent rowboats from Henning's Fishing Station at the foot of the Atlantic Beach bridge. It was the summer I was working as a veterinarian's assistant. I begged my parents to loan me the money for the motor, promising them I would pay them back out of my earnings. I put in $100 and they advanced me another $200 and I was good to go. Only problem was, I found fishing much more fun than working for that vet. So, my poor folks never got their money back. I got myself fired and went fishing instead.

Forty years later, I actually bought a boat of my own. A friend of ours, Mac, took Ariel and me to a boat show in Connecticut where I was a kid again. I got to walk around on many different brands of boats – Sea Rays and Boston Whalers, Sea Pros and Makos – the stuff dreams are made of. Eventually, I ended up sitting on a beautiful little 22-foot Pursuit. It was an open, center-console with a raised front deck, a perfect platform for fly fishing which was, by then, my passion. Although the boat was sitting in a parking lot I was already at sea catching striped bass from the forward deck with a fly rod, making perfect casts to rising fish.

Ariel first knew that we were buying a boat for real when I sat on my Pursuit and didn't get off for an hour or so. It was a big family decision to invest in a boat, but she knew that my heart had been in fishing since I was a boy. When it came time to name the boat, each of us quietly, privately knew her name: *Shya's Dream*.

At first, it was quite a learning curve to pilot a boat. I took a safe boating course offered by the Coast Guard. Then my friend, Mac, introduced me to the concept of "dock and goes" where we tossed a floating cushion out in the middle of the bay. Then I would attempt to approach this decoy as if it were an actual dock in different weather conditions until I became proficient at not bumping it or running it over.

Ariel and I didn't live near the water so we settled for Zuley's, a little marina down on the Jersey shore that was the closest to our home. It sat near the mouth of the Raritan River, near Staten Island and it was only a short hop to the Ocean.

Zuley's is on the edge of a little tidal creek and in the beginning I had to time my departure and return times for when the tide was not rushing in or out, slack tide. This restricted our coming and going to approximately one half hour out of every six. I was determined to master docking my boat in all conditions, so I spent many hours learning to compensate for the effects of the tide and wind on my craft. I was very proud of myself as I moved from novice captain to one who was able to maneuver my way during all types of weather and water conditions.

Four years later, we were up in Cape Cod and I sat on a new boat. It was a 28-foot Contender. And so the process began again. It was time for an upgrade. We soon became the proud owners of an "elderberry" colored boat. Actually, it was a dark creamy pink, but probably the manufacturer thought most men wouldn't purchase a boat in pink so they gave it a fancy name. We named this one, *Dream On*.

At this point in time, I still docked my boat at Zuley's. They had mooring slips on both sides of the tidal creek and I had my boat on a floating dock next to the main boat ramp and the marina itself. On weekends, there is a lot of traffic in and out of the marina and the owners hired Dick, a retired New Jersey State policeman, to sit near the dock, collect ramp fees and direct people where to park their cars and trailers for the day. Dick was actually a rather accomplished captain himself, but his health was somewhat fragile and I think it confined him to the shore more than he would have preferred. However, he was very good at helping nervous captains navigate the ramp, particularly when the tide was rushing.

One Saturday afternoon, I was backing my boat into my boat slip and Dick was sitting nearby. It was a tricky maneuver but by now I was very skilled at compensating for the water's speed and the wind's push, able to slip around other boats and the protruding dock. Dick hurried down to my assistance. He began shouting instructions and rushing to my aid. Frankly, in that moment, I found his "assistance" an intrusion. It was a distraction from the tricky docking procedure I was attempting to undertake. Dick had no idea that I had made this move many, many times and that it was a source of pride for me how well I could execute the maneuver.

I told Dick I didn't need his help. It came out more terse than I intended. Pride collided with pride. Dick may have been a big man, six foot two and 250lbs, but inside he was a sensitive youngster. I hurt his feelings. Dick didn't even realize how upset he was, but it eventually became apparent.

As I left the dock that day, I apologized for growling. "Humph" or something like that was the reply. Neither of us knew at that time that this was the beginning of a battle of wills that would last two years.

I didn't see much of Dick for the rest of the season. I typically led seminars on the weekend and tried to do most of my boating during the week when things were less crowded in the bay. Since Dick only worked on Saturday and Sunday, we had very little interaction that year.

The next year, my boat and I occupied another slip across the tidal creek, directly across from the boat ramp and Dick. One Saturday morning, early in the season, I came down to the marina and realized it was cold and rough outside. I wasn't too sure that I wanted to spend much time out in the choppy water, but since I had a new fly rod, I thought I would practice a little casting off of my dock. Perhaps the weather and the waves would calm down in the meantime.

I was startled to hear a voice shouting from the other side, "Hey, get off the dock!"

I looked up and it was Dick. I shouted back, "Don't worry, Dick, it's me, Shya. I'm allowed to be here. This is my slip."

"No, get off the dock. Zuley doesn't want anyone up there."

"This is my boat and my boat slip. Zuley says it's fine, really." I hollered back. "Give Zuley a call and she'll tell you it's fine."

"No, get off the dock now or I'm calling the police!"

I could see he was very agitated and I decided to cut my losses and head for home. As I pulled out of the parking lot, I saw a police cruiser pulling in. Dick was upset, all right.

The next day I called Zuley.

"Hey," I said, "Can you explain to Dick that it's OK for me to be on the dock? He was very upset with me yesterday and actually called the police when I was leaving because he thought I was trespassing."

Zuley apologized for the confusion and promised to talk with Dick.

The next weekend, the scene repeated itself. No police this time, but he yelled in my direction. I simply headed to my boat and out on the water.

I called Zuley again. This time it was more of a complaint.

"Zuley, can you please talk with Dick. He was harassing me when I came down to my boat."

"I'm sorry," she said, "He can get territorial. He's like an old guard dog. I'll talk with him."

It didn't matter what she said. Dick was like a dog with a bone and he wouldn't let go. Zuley tried writing me a special pass for the dock, taping a permit to the bumper of my car, but to no avail. She couldn't fire him because he was reliable in other ways and she needed him. I began to come to the marina strictly during the week.

The following year, my boat slip was once again back on the marina side, near the boat ramp and near Dick. I tried different tactics to solve the situation. I tried apologizing. I thought if I told him I was sorry we could put this misunderstanding behind us and, if not be friends, at least be cordial. Dick wasn't interested. He claimed to have nothing going on with me. So basically, I nodded to him when coming and going but confined myself to that.

Soon, strange things began happening by my boat. There were mooring ropes that I used to secure my boat to the dock. These ropes were much longer than I needed so I coiled the extra next to the dock cleats. It looked crisp and kept the lines from being tangled and tripped over. However, there were many mornings when I would find the lines in disarray, dangling in the water.

What a nuisance, I thought, and I would coil them up neatly once again on the dock. But they never stayed that way for long.

Eventually I began to notice a pattern. If I went out on a Monday, and went boating again on another weekday such as Thursday, my lines would be neat and coiled just like I had left them. However, when I came to the boat after a weekend, the lines were always kicked in the water, growing brown from silt and sea life.

I suspected it was Dick, but it seemed so petty. He was a grown man after all. Perhaps it was kids coming by, or Zuley's young grandchild. I decided to give Dick the benefit of the doubt and keep my suspicions to myself.

The next time I went to the dock, I brought my drill and some screws. After neatly coiling the lines, I secured them with a few screws and figured that this would make the lines less likely to be inadvertently kicked into the water and less attractive for a youngster to mess around with. But it wasn't long before the lines were ripped up, kicked around and in the water again.

This was not fun. It felt like someone had a vendetta with me. It definitely didn't seem random. It felt more personal. Could it be Dick after all?

Then one Sunday morning, I made it to the marina shortly after Dick had unlocked the gates, just as he was setting up his chair and sun umbrella, getting ready for his day. Once again the ropes were tossed in the water, but this time there was a difference. They were still coiled. They hadn't been in the water long enough to straighten out. I knew I had the culprit. It was the next best thing to catching him in the act.

Once again I went to Zuley. "This is getting ridiculous," I complained. "Boating is supposed to be fun and relaxing and not stressful like this. I feel like I'm in a war zone."

Zuley defended Dick and I understood. If she really saw that he was vandalizing my dock area, she might have to fire him and then she would need to find someone new and Dick, with all of his experience, would be hard to replace.

"I can't believe he would be so juvenile," she said. "He used to be a state cop!"

"But Zuley, that line hadn't been in the water more than ten minutes and he had just unlocked the boatyard with his key. Can't you just talk with him and ask him to leave me alone!"

She said she would. I sincerely hoped that things would ease after that, now that he had been clearly implicated in the trouble. Sad to say, I was mistaken.

The next time I went to take *Dream On* out for a spin, I came down to the boatyard on a Thursday. It was a quiet day. I looked forward to some rest and rejuvenation from our busy schedule. It was low tide and I walked down the ramp and once again my lines were in disarray. *OK*, I thought. *I'll just have to get used to it.* I had tried everything I knew. I had apologized, complained, ignored, avoided and still we were at odds.

As I set my gear on the dock and prepared to board the boat I noticed something strange. My boat had a stain. A yellow stain. When I looked closer, I realized that someone had urinated on my boat!

That was the last straw. I no longer felt safe there. What would be next, sugar in the gas tank? I was shaking when I called Ariel on the phone to tell her about the latest in this ongoing saga between Dick and me. We both agreed it was time to bring *Dream On* home because for now, the dream had turned into a nightmare.

For two weeks our boat resided in the boat barn beside our house. I called Zuley and told her to rent my slip to someone else, I could no longer abide going to her marina. At night, the situation would gnaw on me before sleep. Then suddenly, the answer to my puzzling, distressing situation came to me. I knew what I had to do. I needed to apologize, really apologize.

Yes, I had told Dick I was sorry before, but it was to get what I wanted: To get him off my back, out of my hair, away from my boat. I woke up at 4:00 a.m. realizing that Dick takes great pride in his job, his abilities and his responsibilities and I had rebuffed him way back when I wouldn't let him help me with my docking that day. Everything else had grown from this moment. I could be "right" or I could be "alive."

Ariel and I often talk with people about the difference between being right and being alive, and that to be right, even if you are accurate, there is a cost. You have to give up being alive. And if you want to experience being alive, you have to give up being "right." I knew that I was right that Dick shouldn't be messing with my boat, but I could maintain that stance OR really, truly make peace.

I woke Ariel from her sleep to tell her of my realization.

"I know what to do, Ariel. I need to apologize to Dick and really mean it. I need to go there, with my heart open, and apologize for real, whether he accepts it or not. I hurt his feelings. I was unkind. I need to make amends."

17

"I'm glad." she said sleepily, throwing her arm over my chest. "How about we go down there tomorrow? Let's pick him up some local peaches at the farm next door as a gift."

The next day, we got a half-bushel of peaches and hitched up the boat and trailer to our Suburban and headed down to Zuley's. It was a hot day and when we arrived Dick was standing on the dock, talking with a friend. I took a deep breath and got out of the car. Resting the box of peaches on her hip, Ariel accompanied me on my mission.

Dick glared at me as I walked up. I said to him "Dick, I would like to talk with you, I really owe you an apology." With a surprised look, Dick's friend walked away, giving us privacy. Dick appeared shocked and skeptical, but I continued.

"I behaved like a horse's behind and I'm really sorry for all the grief I've caused you with Zuley. I know you're doing a great job around here and the last thing you need is someone like me giving you grief. I would really appreciate it if you would accept my apology."

"You know," he said. "It takes a big man to admit when he's wrong." And he extended his big hand. I clasped it and he gave me a firm shake. "You should have told me you had permission to be on the dock that time. I would have understood."

I realized then that Dick didn't remember the originating event. He didn't even remember how, in his opinion, I had snubbed him. His memory of events was different than mine. I knew I could tell him that I had told him I had permission to be on that dock, but he hadn't wanted to listen. I knew it was the truth, but I also knew that it would just reignite the fires of unrest and I was ready for peace.

"You're right, Dick." I said. "Again, I'm sorry."

"Forget it," he replied.

I took the box from Ariel. She had been a witness to the event and was quietly holding the gift. If he had rejected my apology we would have taken the peaches back home because they were truly meant as a gift and not as a pay-off to facilitate a truce.

"I have a peace offering for you. Our neighbor grows the most delicious peaches. These are for you."

Dick took the box. He put them on the front seat of his car and told us his girlfriend would make some pies. We asked him where he would like us to park once we put our boat in the water and he indicated a place. For the first time in two years, we went down to our boat fully at peace with Dick and the boatyard.

A funny thing happened for the rest of that season. Our lines remained neatly coiled on the dock.

I imagine Dick's pie tasted very sweet.

IDA

As told by Ariel

Ida was no longer breathing. The artery in her neck still pulsed steadily and I leaned in, calmly watching her lips turn blue. I knew it would only be a few more moments...

Shya's mother, Ida, had been in and out of the hospital for some time. At age 84 her doctor had likened her heart to a tire that was old and worn; it was ready to blow at any time. Max, Shya's father, had understandably been very upset by that analogy. Although this comparison might have been insensitive, I felt the doctor was trying his best to prepare Max for the inevitable. I'm not surprised I wasn't as upset as Max was by the doctor's comments. Ida wasn't my wife and I hadn't spent 64 years of my life with her.

For more than 50 of those 64 years Max and Ida had been working together. As a young bookkeeper, Ida had spotted Max who was then a young cutter in New York City's garment district. A cutter is someone who lays out the patterns over layers of material and then cuts the shapes to be sewn. On the day Max asked her for a date, I'm told that she agreed to go out with him provided he would bring her a pattern of one of the hot new spring dresses. Max fulfilled the request and it was the beginning of a long and fruitful relationship.

I sometimes wonder what Ida did with that pattern. I mean, honestly, sewing wasn't one of her strong suits. By the time I met her, she was embellishing sweaters by appliquéing diamond shaped swatches of material in contrasting color to the front, bordering the patches with bric-a-brac of yet another color and then she would finish the job by sewing in a designer label. Ida had an amazing array of hats, sweaters and the like which I am sure Bill Blass, Scaasi, Vera Wang and Carolina Herrara would have cringed to see their names upon.

Her decline had taken a number of years. At first, it wasn't so obvious. When she was 80, Ida still worked two days a week in New York City as the bookkeeper at the Max Kane Dress Company where Max made designer dresses, wedding and ball gowns.

The shifts in Ida's health and mental state are frozen in slide-like time segments of factory life. Although from time-to-time they came and visited us at our home, we most often saw them at what Ida and Max had come to call "the place."

On one such visit, Ida thoroughly surprised us by asking, "What do you need? If you need money for anything, just let me know and I'll help you. Just don't tell Mr. Kane." She always called Max "Mr. Kane" at the factory, even to us.

The offer for money was quite a shock to Shya. Never in his life had she made such an offer. When he grew up, money had been very tight and the first clothes he ever owned that were not second hand were bought with money he earned himself at age 15. Spartan spending when buying clothes was only the tip of the iceberg when it came to Ida's way with money, but I'll get to that later.

We took Ida up on her offer. She helped us buy our first used car, a pale yellow 1984 Volkswagen Rabbit that ran like a gem for more than ten years. She also helped us buy our first used computer, a big old clunky thing that launched us into the computer age. We were grateful for the assistance, and we honored her request not to tell Mr. Kane.

During some of our weekly visits to the place, Ida often chatted about business and talked about different orders. But suddenly, she would start talking about a designer that Max hadn't worked for in ten or 15 years, as if it were current news. It was as if an old record player needle had mysteriously skipped grooves and was back playing the previous song. Time was no longer progressing linearly for Ida. We got concerned about her ability to keep the books which seemed to be more and more stressful for her. During this time, she and Shya had a frank conversation.

The rows of sewing machines hummed and vibrated in the background as we sat in her little office under the florescent light. "Mom, I'm concerned about something," he began. "What if you become sick or incapacitated? Who will know about your finances? Does Dad know what stocks you have or where the accounts are held?"

The answer was no. Ida had been very secretive over the years but stock dividend checks came to the house regularly. She then kept rubber bands around the pile of used envelopes, "because," she said, "you never knew when you might need scrap paper." Now, at the factory, Ida took a big sheet of pattern paper and drew some grids and her list of assets. It looked like a lot was missing but it was a start.

Soon, Ida started staying home most of the time. The city was too far, her health was failing and she started losing her balance and falling. Luckily, Max at 5'3" was still strong enough to lift her since he had worked hard all his life. But he worried for her safety when he was gone, so he hired daytime help to keep her company and keep her safe.

Ida's physical decline, which had led inexorably to this hospital bed, had been at times graceful and at other times difficult and painful. For instance, it was painful for a formerly self-sufficient person to stop driving. No one wanted to tell her to stop, to take away that freedom. Finally, she mistook reverse for park and thinking she had parked the car, she got out. The car reversed, the door knocked her over as it rolled backward, and it was time. She never drove again.

She hated giving up the bookkeeping but she was no longer able to make the computations. At Ida's insistence, Max brought work home for her at first, but soon she would get agitated and fretful so he stopped and got a bookkeeper in the city. Before long, it was time for another honest conversation. Oh, these talks could be difficult! How do you talk to a parent, or anyone for that matter, about their mortality, their failing health and diminishing mental capabilities. This is not something most of us are trained to do. I am sure my parents felt similarly when they had to broach subjects that were embarrassing or agitating to me as I was growing up. Yes, the roles were finally and irrevocably reversing. We were now operating as parents, acting in what we hoped was Ida's best interest as she was rapidly assuming the role of child.

"Mom, we need to sort out your finances," Shya bravely said on the phone one day. "Where do you keep your stock certificates and records?"

She fidgeted, hemmed and hawed, but eventually she told us they were at home, in the freezer. I immediately imagined stock certificates frozen in blocks of ice and phrases like "cool cash" and "frozen assets." We knew we were out of our depth. It would take someone more knowledgeable than we were, to help sort things out. So we enlisted the aid of our accountant friend, Josh Blau, to come with us and raid Ida's fridge.

We arrived that day and we were all in for a few surprises. Surprise number one: Ida was calm and unperturbed about what we were about to do. She had either accepted that it was time to let go, or her mental process had slipped another notch and she no longer had a grasp on why we were there. I wasn't fond of sitting on the plastic slip covers Ida used to protect the living room furniture, so I asked her to join me in the dining nook to have a chat.

But when Shya and Josh checked the freezer, they discovered surprise number two: The freezer was bare. Had she hidden things? Was this a new game of hide and seek? Ida appeared guileless. It was time to hunt.

I thought about being young, when my sisters and I would hide something and one of us would look for the concealed object. The person who had camouflaged the item would give feedback as we searched, "You are getting warmer, warmer, hotter," etc. if we moved toward the hiding place or "You are getting cold, colder, ice cold," as we moved away.

Well, the freezer was pretty warm, but not the actual stashing spot. Next to the freezer was an old brown shopping bag. This bag was hot, red hot. In this bag was years and years of accumulated financial information.

Sorting through this brown paper safety deposit box turned out to be a dangerous mission. Ida had unwittingly, booby-trapped the bag to would-be intruders. Ida didn't see the need to buy paper clips since she had an endless supply of straight pins from her clothing factory. Many times, Josh withdrew his hand from this grown-up version of a grab bag and the record would automatically come along, its pin embedded in his finger or thumb.

Old crumbled bits of doilies, linoleum, fabrics and old, old stock certificates, like Studebaker, still lived in that bag. There were other bags there, too. Suddenly things began to come clear. Envelopes and rubber bands were not the only things that Ida had collected. There in those bags, unbeknownst to her children or even Mr. Kane, Ida had amassed a veritable fortune. Max was shocked.

"She still gets upset when I buy Minute Maid Orange Juice instead of a store brand," was his comment that I remember most.

A piece of the puzzle had fallen into place and a picture was starting to emerge. Now I knew why Ida never wanted us to tell Mr. Kane about those previous gifts. She hadn't wanted him to suspect she had money to spend.

It was months later, in the hospital that day, as I sat at her bedside, watching her lips grow blue. The moment was here. I held Ida's hand and leaned directly into her line of sight so that my face was positioned close in front of hers. It was important that she knew she was not alone. Here it came, the gasp, the reflexive gripping of my hand as Ida returned from her journey, sucking in a panicked breath as her body, not quite ready to relinquish its hold, reasserted its need for oxygen.

I had been with Ida for several hours now. She would stop breathing, journey off and then return with the terror of one who is starved for air. Her system was sending the equivalent of alarms and bells and whistles. "You are suffocating!" it would scream and she would return with a start, in fear for her life. I had no fear for her and it showed in my expression and demeanor. So I put my face in her path and it would be the first image she would catch sight of. My calm would then infuse her.

See, I knew in my heart that Ida was terrified of dying. I also knew that each trip she was making, now, was like a trial run and that my presence could melt the fear and ease her passing. And in so doing I earned many gifts. I got to see the wonder in her eyes as she returned and focusing on my gaze, love was in her face. Sometimes, when she re-emerged to consciousness, she would repeat the same sentence over and over. I began to see that many of these were unresolved concerns left over from long ago which had stayed with her. Others were stories or events of which she was proud and which she needed to share. And I was the vessel, the fortunate recipient of these gifts. Shya was, too, of course, because he was there in the room, but I loved being with Ida in this way, so he gave me space.

Clutching my hand, Ida lurched back to this reality. Disoriented for a minute she tried to raise up to get more air. I am familiar with this feeling. It is not one of my favorites. Sometimes, while meaning to swallow, I actually inhale my saliva instead and my throat closes; feeling like I can't breathe, it is hard to relax and not panic. But relaxing was exactly what I was training Ida to do.

I am so pleased to see you back, my look said.

Her look had an intensity. *There is something I have to tell you*, it replied.

As I listened as intently as I knew how, she said, "You have no idea what it is like to be dependent on money and then lose it. I swore I would never become dependent on money again!" There was a pleading in her eyes. *Don't judge me!* they entreated.

More pieces of the puzzle gently floated into place. Of course, many families go through tight times and have to watch their pennies to make ends meet, but with Ida, conserving money had always been a top priority. When Shya was 13, his older sister, Sandra, got a lump on her neck. "Just a swollen gland," the doctor said. For six months this "gland" stayed swollen and grew in size but no more trips to the doctor were scheduled, no second opinions asked for. Doctors cost money, after all. Finally, finally, they went again. But, by now, it was too late. Sandra had spinal cancer and she eventually succumbed to the disease, dying at age 24, seven long years later.

The decision to delay further action on Sandra's lump had embittered some family members. But as I sat with this fragile old lady, holding her hand, I realized that at some moment in time when she was young, Ida had made herself a solemn oath to conserve money, however large a sacrifice it might seem. She had made this promise to herself, never even glimpsing what the future might have in store, and she had paid the ultimate price.

"It's not right for a parent to outlive her children," she had told me more than once.

I smiled down at her tenderly. *I love you. I forgive you. It's all right, you can rest now.*

Soon Ida begin to slide in and out of consciousness with more and more ease. Today would not be the day of her death but it was coming. I could feel it. All she had were a precious few days.

Around ten days later, Ida was back in Intensive Care. She would not be going home again. She was drifting in and out like before, her breathing stopping, her neck pulsing, but by now the process was infinitely easier and simpler. Her eyes would remain open, her gaze fixed, and she would just go. When she came back, each return was new and fresh and alive. It went something like this: As Ida regained awareness of her surroundings, Shya said,

"Hello, Ida. Did you have a nice journey?"

"Oh yes," she replied with enthusiasm. "It was beautiful!"

She smiled, her wrinkled old face and sunken eyes appearing beatific. Then her countenance relaxed and she was away again, her gaze still looking at me but she wasn't there. I held her hand and waited. Shya and I had our faces pressed side-by-side so she could see us both when she re-emerged.

Sometimes she came back a bit disoriented but always, always she was so happy to see us.

"Oh, it's you!" she would exclaim. "I love you so much," and then she would go, only to return again, surprised and delighted to see us once more, "Oh, it's you, I love you so much!" Each return was new. She was new and so were we.

At one point she stayed lucid for a longer stretch of time. Taking Shya's hand, she gave him the equivalent of a dying sage's blessing.

"You know, I must admit, Shya, that when you were younger, I never thought you would turn out, but you did. I am very proud of you."

Wow, what a gift! We all cried as Shya and she held hands. Then she drifted away. When she came back, Ida looked him in the eye and said, "You are going to be very famous some day," and she left again.

Ida was in a rhythm of her own now. Her body was closing itself down bit by bit. Her race was almost run.

Two nights later, Ida finally slipped away for good. She was laid to rest in a beautiful mahogany casket that Rhoda, Shya's sister, had picked out. Before the service, we and the family met with the Rabbi. "This is a sad day," he said as we passed the tissues and snuffled into hankies. "But, it is also a day where you can share stories about Ida Speiler who got married and became Ida Kane. These stories are a legacy which should be preserved and handed down to your children."

To get the ball rolling, he asked Ruth, Ida's only remaining sibling, to tell a little of Ida's early life. Ruth, a tiny almost replica of her sister, stood in front of the Rabbi's desk and recited some facts of old that were new to us.

"Ida was born on Rivington Street near Delancy," she began. These streets were on Manhattan's lower east side. This we already knew. "Things were pretty normal at first and then the depression came. My father lost his job. Everyone was out of work and Ida got a job and supported the whole family. She was 13, then."

I got a rush as if someone had poured ice water over my head. The hairs raised on my arms. Of course. Now the puzzle was completed. I imagined a petite child of 13, laboring to feed her siblings and both parents. She had to support Harry, Eddy, Ruth, Matt, her mother, her father, and herself, seven in all.

"You have no idea what it is like to be dependent on money and then lose it," she had said. "I swore I would never become dependent on money again!"

Later during the service, I offered my own silent prayer, *Oh, Ida, Ida. I understand. I am so, so sorry. Things must have hurt really badly. I have such compassion for you. I love you so much. I hope now you can finally rest in peace.*

DISSOLVING MECHANICAL BEHAVIORS

We all have mechanical behaviors, those ways of relating to life that crop up over and over – the "bad" habits that plague us. What if simple awareness (seeing something without judging it or judging yourself) were enough to dissolve this unwanted conduct?

A mechanical behavior is usually something that we put together when we were young, as a strategy for survival or success. It may even have been a strategy to get attention. It worked once, or so we thought, but it no longer supports us in having a satisfying life. Mechanical behaviors can also be learned; passed down through the generations as a familial way of relating to life. These ways of being are frozen in time and replay again and again, and we are seemingly powerless to correct them.

If you like, you can think of a mechanical behavior as a block of ice, and awareness as the sun. In these chapters, you will find the heat to melt even the most stubborn of habits.

A CLUTTERED DESK IS A SIGN OF GENIUS
As told by Ariel

Ever since Shya and I began to lead seminars, I've been amazed that everywhere we traveled, from Hawaii to Bali, Indonesia, from Germany to Chile, from Holland to Costa Rica, I could easily reconstruct my desk to resemble the one at home. Papers and things that needed to be done would wait for me in piles, often getting shunted from pile to pile and back again. I still was very productive. I did things well and on time but it was as if my desk and I were combatants, on opposing teams playing a game of fetch or hide and seek.

My earliest memories of my desk are from, well, my earliest memories. My childhood desk was painted white and red with a piece of glass covering the entire top, under which my parents helped me put photos. This photo gallery included pictures of my family and me at the beach, me and my kindergarten sweetheart, Stevie Emerick, at Blue Lake Park, school photos, and later, goofy snapshots of my best friend Terri Rickert and me. But one thing remained a constant in my childhood and adolescence; you could rarely see the photos on my desktop. They were always covered with the detritus of day-to-day life.

I don't recall working much at this desk. I generally did my home-work in the kitchen. Nor do I recall sitting much at this desk. It was primarily a horizontal surface, a catchall for items flung down in passing, stuffed animals out of favor and clothes already worn.

Later in life, I would admonish myself for not being better organized. Then, when I started attending seminars as a participant in my early twenties, I re-contextualized the general mess. I am well organized, I told myself. This is just my style of organization.

And so it went… this background of general desk clutter that followed me from home to home, country to country, location to location.

One Christmas, Shya and I went to visit my parents in my childhood home. The house was immaculate, as usual, and I found a marble plaque in one of the upstairs bedrooms that read: *A Cluttered Desk is a Sign of Genius.* It made me smile. I felt right at home reading this sentiment. What a great justification for being me.

I went downstairs to the kitchen and poured a cup of coffee. As I joined my mom at the kitchen table where she was working on a crossword puzzle, I said, "What a great little plaque you have upstairs, *A Cluttered Desk is a Sign of Genius.*"

Looking over the top of her reading glasses she replied, "I had it in my office for years. Guess who gave it to me?"

"Me?"

"Yes, you."

Then I remembered. When I was about 13, I had found the plaque at the local card store and I thought it fit my mother's desk at the *Glass Butterfly*, the clothing store my parents owned in my hometown, Gresham, Oregon. Her office always intrigued me. It was rather small and square but it felt like the heart of the store. The door was inset with frosted etched glass, my mother had an antique wrought iron free standing coat rack, and then there was her desk. It was big and L-shaped and covered with piles of orders, files, correspondence and stuff. The mountainous topography of her desktop was mysterious and impressive. There were numerous occasions when I heard her say, "Don't move anything. I know right where to lay my hands on the things I want."

My parents had been retired from business for a several years but they kept some of the antiques like the coat rack and the marble plaque from a younger me.

"Take it home with you if you like," she said. "You can have it."

That Christmas I got an extra gift which I lovingly tucked in my suitcase, wrapped in a muffler to prevent damage. I gave it a place of honor on my very own desk.

When Shya had his arthroscopic knee surgery, I had plenty of quiet time. Our office, an open loft space, is right above our bedroom. Since Shya was in his first days back from the hospital, I moved around on ghostly feet and didn't turn on music, the TV or talk much on the phone. As I moved from space to space in our home, I realized that each room was what I'd call psychically quiet. I take great pleasure in completing things so I don't talk to myself about what needs to get done as I pass by a doorway.

In other words, the massage table in the session room had a clean sheet covering it and the guest bedroom was ready to receive guests. This way I don't need to be pulled by my thoughts when I move through my home. Of course, there is the ebb and flow of day-to-day living, the dishes and dust, the laundry and such. But in general, things always get done or are moving towards getting done, everywhere – except in my office. Now, with Shya recovering from surgery, I was handling the things we normally did together seamlessly and effortlessly. The mystery of my office suddenly had been painted in bright colors by circumstance.

I made tea and soup, moving through my day, quietly contemplating the state of my office and more specifically my desk. Here is what I knew: There weren't piles all of the time. I completed most things each year before we left to teach our winter residential courses in Costa Rica or Chile. I often straightened things up before going away to teach in Germany or California for a week or two, and from time-to-time I would do an office purge, cleaning files and completing everything on top of my desk. But empty horizontal spaces never lasted long. The piles quickly accumulated once again and soon the clutter was back.

I've spent enough time getting to know myself and supporting others to no longer buy the story I had told myself, *This is just my style of organizing.* I usually didn't worry about the state of my desk because I had come to accept that this was the way it was and picking on myself did nothing to alleviate things. Still, in the privacy of my own thoughts, I wondered why my desk was cluttered.

Truth be told, I had plenty of half-formed theories. These are the old ideas I had tried on in the past, like an ill fitting coat, as a way of blaming myself and explaining away that which I seemed powerless to change. The first theory, perhaps my oldest, went something like: I am L-A-Z-Y. The next was the convenient, blame your mom garden variety: I learned it from my mother; it's not my fault. Later, I came up with more sophisticated ideas: I like to be in control and the clutter is my way of making sure that I'm the only person to handle the office work. Or, I don't like to be told what to do, even by the papers on my desk that demand my attention.

I placed some tea and a snack for Shya on a tray so I could serve him in bed while my thoughts rummaged through my list of reasons for my cluttered desk. I was beginning to realize that when folks came to our home, I wanted them to feel as warm and welcomed in my office as they were elsewhere. I knew that most people didn't judge my clutter and often times it didn't even register with them as a mess, but I was tired of feeling apologetic when someone came up into the room where I spend a lot of my time.

Turning sideways to accommodate my tea tray, I made my way through the doorway as I carefully brought the food and drink to Shya. Groggy from the pain medication, he sat up in bed. It was really good to see him. I was surprised at my eagerness to have a casual conversation and share my day with him. I perched on the corner of the mattress.

"I've been thinking of the office and my desk and wondering why it's so messy," I said.

He paused, leaned back looking thoughtful and said, "I see two things."

"Oh good, you tell me your ideas, then I'll tell you mine!" I quickly responded.

"Well," he said, "you're going too fast, trying to get things done so you're not fully where you are. That's the first thing. Also, it has to do with that marble plaque you have up there."

"OK, that's two, but you missed one," I replied without missing a beat. I trotted out my current best theory, "I think I like to be in control and this is my way to keep you out of the office and have it all to myself."

Shya, to his credit, didn't laugh at me. Nor did he get irritated. He simply sighed, cocked his head to one side and said, "You know it's funny that this problem is following you around and you want to tell me why you have this problem rather than listen to what I have to say."

Uh-oh! I had seen plenty of people in our seminars with a pet problem, one that plagued them forever. But when Shya, other participants or I gave suggestions or feedback, they would quickly tell us, "No, here is my theory…" Coming up with an "I know that already and that's not it" attitude effectively defends them from having to hear anything new or really listen to anything at all. I am aware in those moments that people may say they want to resolve something but if a habit has been with them for a long time, it's like an old friend, one that they are often reluctant to say good-bye to, regardless of what they tell themselves. No matter how bothersome the habit, people often vigorously defend it by being "right" about the reason they have the habit in the first place. I could recall experience after experience of how a person's "bad" habit is actually kept in place by the reasons or theories he or she has for its existence.

I took a deep breath and felt an involuntary shudder. I guess I was ready to listen, really listen this time.

"OK, start over please," I said.

"When you pick up a piece of paper, you're not really there with it. You're already onto the next thing, trying to get it all done. If you could slow down just a little bit, you would complete a lot more things."

This made sense. Sometimes a magazine would want us to advertise or a company would ask us if we wanted to display books with them for upcoming book shows. Or an offer from a new car insurance company would cross my desk. For these types of things, if I didn't have an immediate answer, I would set them aside for later, sometimes much later, so I could get on to "important" things. Shya gently added, "The biggest thing is that plaque up there. You should get rid of it. You're married to sentimentality, doing it the way you devised when you were a child."

Ah, how true. I had been battling this "problem" for at least 40 years. I thanked Shya. Thanking me in return, he finished his snack and settled back down to sleep, recuperating from his knee surgery. Now I had food for thought.

I took a leap of faith. I put aside my ideas and tried on his as if they were true. And a really, truly amazing thing happened: *Instantaneous Transformation*. Really.

After I cleared the dishes, I went up into the office and quietly sat down at my desk. I picked up the top piece of paper and actually read it. As I worked my way through the pile, I saw many outdated things, which I recycled. I created files for others and put them away. I called the people who needed reaching. I handled each thing as I came to it. And amazingly, it was easy. It was effortless. Even more amazing, I was no longer trying to clean my desk or get things done. I simply applied myself with totality and engaged without preference. Time lost its hold over me. Over the next few days, I found myself creating solutions for things that had plagued me for years. Horizontal surfaces reappeared. And still, the plaque, *A Cluttered Desk is a Sign of Genius*, sat on my desk.

Privately, I thought perhaps I could transcend its message. Maybe I could think of something superior to being a genius and aspire toward that. I didn't want to lose the hard earned connection between my mom and me after those heated teenage years. Thoughts flitted around in my awareness.

I began to realize that childhood love, emulation and loyalty to one's parents is a complex, mysterious, wonderful thing that can move forward in time until aspects of it are no longer appropriate.

I realized that my memories of my mother's organizational style was skewed to fit the reality I had as a young person when I mentally recorded events. I have seen lots of folks only remember those things that fit with their theories of life. So even if it had worked for Mom to pile things up, it didn't mean I was deserting her if it didn't work for me. These thoughts came and went and through it all I steadily, effortlessly completed item after item, project after project.

My desk is made of wood. I currently have a clear plastic blotter under which I have placed pictures, kind of like in the old days. Only now I get to enjoy them on a regular basis. I still occasionally call my friends to let them know that I'm sitting at my beautiful, clean desk in my beautiful, organized office.

My life transformed in an instant. Of course, there were things to be done but it was almost as if they completed themselves, I just needed to get out of the way. I finally learned that a cluttered desk is not a sign of genius. It is a sign of clutter. And for me it signaled a need to slow down and be where I was rather than trying to do it right and get ahead.

About that plaque – I originally thought I should give it to Goodwill or The Salvation Army, pass it on so to speak. But then I felt badly about giving another person a reason to keep his or her clutter. I let our assistant, Christina, take it away and I believe it went out in the trash. From time-to-time I get a pang of nostalgia and think I should have kept it. Then I realize that I don't really miss it and I don't want to keep reinforcing something that is no longer me.

How wonderful that my mother gave me back my gift to her. More wonderful still is the fact that it became a trigger for me to really look at my life. I realize today that I don't need to live by what amused me and intrigued me as a child. I also know that my connection with my mother is made stronger by being me, not in resistance to her or by emulating a child's idea of who she was.

COMING FULL 'IRCLE

What if you are doing your life perfectly? What if the things that you think are failings on your part are not really failings at all? Has it ever occurred to you that as a child you perfectly absorbed information from your environment, learning wholeheartedly when your brain was not yet able to discern truth from fiction nor to apply reason and thought?

Our friends Amy and Andy have a beautiful little boy, Alex. We were privileged to be at the hospital when he was born and have watched him on his journey from infancy to early childhood.

At the ripe old age of 22 months, you could see that Alex had learned many things, demonstrating that he clearly knew the difference between hard and soft. When Alex wanted to express his displeasure at not getting his way (like being asked to eat the Cheerios from a small baggie rather than from the big box he wanted to hold) he would throw himself on the floor in an impressive display of histrionics. The velocity of Alex's descent to the floor depended on which room of the house he was in during his melt-down. In the family room, he did a full-fledged flop since the floor has thick carpeting. But Alex was more cautious on the wood floors and avoided landing on stone if he could help it. One time, he got upset while he was on the brick walkway leading to the front door. He prepared himself for a full tilt fit but managed to stop the action before hitting brick. He actually picked himself up and walked the few feet to the cushy welcome mat before "spontaneously" throwing himself down to cry.

Yes, Alex had learned well and his little boy mind had collected all sorts of useful information, causing him to feel passionately about many things. When Alex was 15 months old he discovered circles. For some time, Alex was like an investigative reporter, on the hunt for anything round that he could point out with glee to his parents, and to anyone who would listen. "'ircle!" Alex would shout. It seems that while his brain was able to identify the shape, his mouth could not yet form the "S" sound at the beginning of the word. So instead of being surrounded by circular shapes, Alex's world was inhabited by "'ircles."

Alex could find 'ircles anywhere – the balloon motif around the ceiling at the doctor's office, a clock face, a ball. The MasterCard™ logo once sent Alex into a frenzy when he realized it had two over-lapping 'ircles. It often surprised his parents that round shapes, even if they were simply a part of the background environment, could be spotlighted by Alex's nimble mind. Amy and Andy found the passion their son had for 'ircles endearing. They did however, from time-to-time, feel concerned that Alex couldn't pronounce the word correctly. They could only hope that sooner or later Alex would be able to fix his earlier mistake in pronunciation when his ability to speak caught up with his powers of observation.

One day, while casually leaning on the doorframe watching his son play, Andy had a stunning revelation. Alex was on all fours, rolling a big yellow school bus back and forth, one of his favorite toys. On the side of the bus were four shapes: a triangle, a square, a heart and a circle. Plopping on his behind, Alex pushed the triangle and when the button was depressed, the electronic voice exclaimed, "Triangle!" When Alex hit the square, the voice called out, "Square!" and then he pushed the big round button and the machine hollered, "'ircle!"

Astounded, Andy came into the room, knelt by his son and pushed the button. Again the toy faithfully repeated, "'ircle!" Alex could make the "S" sound. It was not his mistake. He had learned perfectly, and with passion, to say 'ircle instead of circle from a defective toy.

All of us have learned how to behave and relate from things we put together as youngsters or by things we absorbed from our environment. But that was before we had the benefit of discerning whether or not we were getting complete or accurate information.

As you go through life, it's very easy to blame one's parents or teachers or environment and say they were bad role models or deficient in some way. But stop and think. Those people you may seek to blame also learned and absorbed from their environments without their young minds being able to discern truth from fiction or apply reason and thought.

Just the way Andy discovered the defective audio in the toy while watching his son, you can also discover how you function. Casually lean on the doorframe of your life and observe how you operate without judging what you discover. You will be instantaneously empowered to include small details that were omitted. If you can treat yourself with humor, love and respect, much like you would a young child who is learning from his or her environment, you will reclaim your wholehearted nature and passion for living. When you allow yourself to come full 'ircle, and rediscover the art of self-observation without self-reproach, it will have a profound impact on your well-being.

YOU CAN'T SEE ME
As told by Ariel

I was in our office one sunny afternoon, answering emails when I happened to glance out the sliding glass door to the deck. Our office is a second floor loft space and at one end there is a small deck overlooking our back yard with the woods beyond. It is, in general, a peaceful view with the leaves dappled in the sunlight or restlessly tossing about on a windy day.

On this particular afternoon, I saw a sapling shaking wildly, just beyond the perimeter of our lawn. I'm used to the ripples that birds make as they hop from limb-to-limb on the skinny branches or the quivering that accompanies a squirrel as it uses the aerial super highway, jumping from oak-to-oak. But this was a much stronger movement and it caught my eye. I stood, stretched, and moved to the door to survey the scene.

I have always thought that ground hogs were meant to live on the ground as their name implies. However, right there, up in a mulberry tree was a fat football of a ground hog, happily munching the leaves he was stripping from the branches. I snorted a laugh as an old nursery rhyme came to mind, "How much wood could a wood-chuck chuck if a woodchuck could chuck wood?"

I watched the critter's steady progress and eventually thought about how much I wanted this tree to live. If he ate all of the leaves, it was sure to die. I tapped on the glass with my knuckle and immediately the ground hog froze. All chewing ceased. All movement stopped. He dropped into an instinctual survival mode; if he didn't move, I wouldn't see him. Sliding the door open I stepped out on the deck and began talking to my guest.

"What do you think you're doing?"

Moving his head a little to the right, he hid his eyes behind a leaf. I don't know if ground hogs have a logic system but if they do, he surely was thinking, "You can't see me!"

I leaned against the railing for a few moments, amused by his approach. It reminded me of people we've met over the years who discovered something about themselves that they found embarrassing. Immediately they froze up, probably thinking, "If I don't move, maybe nobody will see me being this way."

The funny thing is, the things people hide from themselves have usually been seen all along. Friends and family still love them including the habits or foibles they find embarrassing. It is akin to discovering you have a piece of lettuce caught between your front teeth hours after you ate.

I continued my conversation with Woody woodchuck, "I can still see you. Climb out of my tree please. Come on. Get down."

As he began his wobbly descent I had an idea of how he got up there in the first place. The tree was a sapling that bent to and fro with his weight and it had allowed him to climb the trunk as if it were an uphill balance beam. My furry friend had done an animal high wire act, but getting down wasn't as easy as getting up. Having to turn around was not something he had anticipated. Facing me, he gripped with his four little paws and rocked back and forth, an ungainly gymnast on his wobbly high beam.

Eventually he changed direction, the sapling swung in response and the upper leaves quivered. He safely climbed down from his precarious perch and later in the season you could see him munching on the grass or lounging on our lower deck; all regular activities for ground hogs who generally do not climb trees or perform acrobatics.

Each time I saw him, I remembered that you can't hide from others by hiding behind a leaf. People can see you anyway. Those things that you hide from yourself are usually already seen and known and accepted by those who love you. If you want to dissolve something that you find embarrassing, you can't simply freeze and hope that will handle the problem. If you have compassion for yourself, even if you feel "caught," the simple act of seeing yourself without beating yourself up will help you out of the tree in which you are hiding and allow you to move on to greener pastures.

I'M HUNGRY!
As told by Ariel

When I think I'm hungry, I really am. Right? It can't just be a thought, can it? I mean, I'm familiar with random or negative thoughts that are not rooted in reality. I can recognize those repeated litanies, nasty little recordings that play when one does not meet his or her own expectations. You know, the internal commentary that says, "That was pitiful!" when you miss the wastebasket from two feet away. It's the noisy little voice that says, "I can't ask for a raise," or "he'll never go out with me." But surely this voice doesn't give me directives that are completely and utterly false. Actually, I've discovered that it does.

In the early 90's Shya and I were living in a little house just outside of Woodstock, NY. It was overlooking the Ashokan reservoir, one of the main water supplies for New York City. We did most of our work during the day and at night we often sat down in front of the TV for a little entertainment before bed. It was during this time that I would forage in the kitchen for a little nosh to satisfy my evening cravings.

"I'm hungry," I'd say to myself as I sprung from the couch and headed to the cupboards for a mini meal. This pattern of behavior went on unexamined until one night, Shya and I went out for Indian food.

Tucked away in one of the little valleys between the Catskills was a restaurant that made delicious dishes: red lentil soups, super spicy vindaloo, curry, and saffron rice. Along with tandoori and flat bread stuffed with potato and peas, there were dishes savory and spicy, pickled and chutneyed. Going to this place was a rare treat and when we made the 40-minute drive there, we generally ate our fill and then some.

On this particular Friday night the air was cool, the leaves gently rustling in the evening breeze. The moon was half full and we had a very pleasant drive. When we arrived, you could hear the nearby stream in the background and feel the damp, dewy grass. Inside the restaurant, the walls were rich wood and the smells were heavenly. As soon as we were seated, a waiter brought us flat lentil wafers called papadum with a stainless steal condiment tray filled with three tasty sauces; green herb and yogurt, a red spicy sauce and minced onion relish. We happily began munching as we looked over the menus.

"Mmm," Shya said, "How about some appetizers?"

He didn't have to ask me twice. We decided on vegetable pakoras and onion fritters, both doughy, fried and yummy. We ordered savory lentil soup with spinach, kiln baked bread, vegetable rice, and two main dishes with rich sauces. By the time we were finished, we were stuffed, but there was still the prospect of desert. We loved the flaky philo dough and honey and nut confections so we decided we simply had to share a plate, along with a pot of hot Chai tea.

Truthfully, we completely over indulged and bursting at the seams, we made our way to the car. We got in, making sure the seat belts weren't too tight across our laps. On the drive home we leaned back, contented and let the meal begin to digest.

As we pulled into our driveway, the moon reflected off the water far below and we decided that it would be fun to watch a movie on HBO before bed.

We plopped down on the couch and Shya put his arm around me as we settled back just in time for the 10 o'clock feature. Less than an hour later, I was hungry again. Really hungry. I jumped up and rushed to the refrigerator and stood there, door open, surveying the scene. Do I want apples or pickles or left-overs or...

"Wait a minute!" As I balanced on my two feet that had moved with such alacrity into the kitchen, I looked down at my belly which was still distended from the nights debauchery. Not only was I not hungry, I was stuffed!

Still standing in front of the refrigerator, I slowly closed the door, mentally retracing my trajectory from the couch to the kitchen. What had vaulted me from my seat? What ever had possessed me to even think that I could possibly need a snack? I heard the music from the other room, the movie was still in progress and I got my answer in a flash.

This "problem" of mine of late night eating, was actully a very clever solution. On the television, the tension mounted. The camera angle was close and our hero was in trouble. Any moment now something bad was going to happen. I just knew it. I couldn't bear to watch. I wasn't hungry at all. Getting a bite to eat was my escape. I could avoid the scary parts if I left for the kitchen.

Slowly I wandered back to the living room and actually looked at the thing I was avoiding. Sure enough, the plot thickened and the hero got a scary jolt and so did I. That's the nature of a scary film. I sat back down on the couch and reminded myself that it was just a movie, after all. Smiling a little to myself, I wrapped Shya's arm back around my shoulders and watched as the hero, eventually, saved the day.

I THOUGHT I WAS OVER THAT

People generally work on the things they don't like about themselves, trying to change, fix or get rid of certain aspects of their behavior. When faced with an unwanted, repeating pattern, however, people often think of it as a personal failure.

Many times in our dealings with folks we hear, "Oh, I thought I was over that by now. I'm so much better than I used to be."

There is an anecdote we like to share in such situations. It is from a time in Ariel's childhood and it is told from her point of view:

Brownie, our dog, was barking wildly at the cat. Of course this was nothing new. My sister Mary's little reddish brown toy Cocker Spaniel was a fierce warrior and family protector. Many a time our neighbor, old Mr. Van, would hobble up the hill with a rubber thong on only one foot snorting, "Where is that confounded dog?!" I once actually saw the little furry devil get so excited barking at a car that he buried his teeth in a tire and barely let go in time, as his whole body began to follow the tire's rotation.

When Mary was in second grade she wrote a poem that still lives in my memory because, as her little sister, I thought it was exceedingly clever: "Brownie is the bravest dog I ever knew. He chases the milkman and he even bit Grandma."

Now that you have our family dog's background, it's time to tell you more about when Brownie chased the cat.

It was a dark evening and Brownie had followed the cat, slipping into the garage through a door that was left ajar. Our garage, an old building separate from the house, was mainly a repository for bed frames, wooden skis, gardening tools and the like. Rarely did my parents park a car in there, as the big wooden door was heavy and creaky and not easily lifted.

It was a Thursday night and our family was getting ready to go to a concert at my eldest sister Cathy's Junior High School. She had on a skirt, a white blouse and a beautiful new mohair cardigan sweater hand-knit by my mother. It was cream-colored and fuzzy with shell buttons and I loved it.

"Cathy," my mother said, "please go out to the garage and get Brownie to stop barking at the cat, would you? Bring him inside so we can go." She'd finished braiding my hair and we were almost ready to leave but there were always lots of details to be handled before she could get her young family out the door and to an event on time.

We had many cats over the span of my childhood but if my memory serves, the current pet was called Pepper. This feisty grey and black striped tabby with a loud raspy purr eventually gifted us with a litter of orange striped and black balls of fur. My father led me into the basement one day to let me "discover" the kittens first.

On this night it seemed that Pepper was holding her own. The shrill, "Bark, bark, bark... Bark, bark, bark," relentlessly repeated and got louder in intensity as I followed Cathy to the garage. Brownie's barking didn't skip a beat as the heavy garage door creaked and groaned in protest as Cathy used all her strength to lift it open. The bare bulb on the outside fixture at the apex of the roof sent fingers of light into the musty darkness. It wasn't enough to illuminate much but I could see Brownie furiously expressing his outrage at Pepper whose silhouette was barely visible as she faced him down, wedged between a couple of bikes.

"Come on, Brownie," Cathy coaxed in the semi-bored tone that I adored, since she was such a mature pre-teen and all. But our dog was being particularly stubborn, not knowing we had places to go and a new sweater to show off.

Cathy did not need to reach for the inside light switch as Brownie was clearly, albeit dimly, in view. But in retrospect, I'm sure she wished that she had. As my sister strode forward, leaning in to grab him, Pepper turned tail and presented us her backside. In that moment, both Cathy and I knew why Brownie had been so relentless. The vague light from the doorway caught the thick white stripe down the creature's back and in the wink of an eye, "pfffft." Both Cathy and Brownie were sprayed by a skunk.

We didn't make it to the concert that night. My sister's outfit was buried out back, new sweater and all. Both the dog and she took turns getting bathed in tomato juice, a remedy said to neutralize the stench.

Cathy didn't go back to school until the following Monday as the lingering odor still followed her around. The kids who were blunt, honest and sometimes cruel had plenty to tease her about. "PeeUuu, you stink!" they cried.

Head held high, she quipped, "Oh, I hardly smell at all anymore. You should have smelled me last week."

Perhaps you are proud that you cleaned up an old way of relating or being that you didn't like. But if you assume it is a closed book, a completed chapter, you may not notice the vestiges of stinky behaviors that, from time-to-time, reappear in your life. If you see an old behavior, it may not look, feel (or smell) so good but take a page from Cathy's playbook and hold your head high. Don't worry. If you simply allow yourself to be you, smell and all, without judging yourself, this too shall pass.

HELPING YOURSELF/HELPING OTHERS

People often talk about how they want to change things in their lives; get a better job, have a relationship, lose weight and feel better about themselves. But how can this happen when most of us gather proof to support the limiting story we have told ourselves about who we are? If you are not willing to see yourself through a fresh perspective, devoid of your preconceived shortcomings, your best intentions for growth may not end up the way you wish.

What is possible depends on your willingness to let go of short-sighted ideas and step out into life. If you are looking at things through your inadequacies, you'll have to give up that position in order to discover your potential.

There are some very simple keys to achieve your desires or to back someone else who is going for his or hers. The following pages will support you when lending a hand to another and assist you in going for your dreams.

SAVE ME!

As told by Ariel

One moment Shya was lying next to me, an instant later he was gone...

It was the early 90's in Maui, Hawaii and we were sunning ourselves at one of our favorite spots, Little Beach. It was a beautiful day, warm, sunny and the local clouds had yet to form. The island and hills behind Little Beach are such that most every afternoon, regardless of the weather in the surrounding area, a tendril of clouds gathers and reaches over the beach to point out to sea. We loved going there for the quiet and the white sand. You had to climb from nearby Big Beach, over a rocky hillock and so the area always seemed more private and was populated mostly by locals.

On this particular day, Shya and I had been body surfing the waves. This is an art form I learned there and have rarely practiced elsewhere – standing in water waist deep and diving toward land, just in front of a breaking wave, holding my breath, arms extended as the water's force jettisoned me toward shore, depositing me breathless and sandy in the shallows – an exhilarating game. We had flopped, belly down, on our towels, fat drops of water glistening in the sun as they rolled off our backs, still heaving from the exertion. The next thing I knew, Shya disappeared.

I rolled over and sat up in time to see him sprinting for the ocean, angling to the right and diving into the surf. He resurfaced and long fast strokes took him directly out to sea. It also cut the distance between him and a head bobbing ever farther from shore. I knew immediately what was happening.

As a young man, Shya had been a lifeguard at Far Rockaway Beach in New York City. He had spent several summers scanning the water, not only saving swimmers who underestimated the pull of the surf but heading off trouble before it began. Shya had recognized at a glance that the person in the distance was caught in a riptide, more commonly known as an undertow.

An undertow develops when you have a large volume of water that comes onto a length of shore and then it funnels back out predominantly in one area. If you happen to wander into this area it can be anything from a gentle tugging that nibbles at your ankles to being caught in a river where the current will move you right out into deeper water. Novices to the ways of the surf, will often not realize that they are caught up in an outgoing riptide until they see that they are suddenly much farther from shore than they had expected. Usually, in a panic, they try to swim directly back to the safety of land. The current is too strong for this direct approach and people make little headway, get tired and then, without assistance, often times, drown. A seasoned ocean swimmer will know that an undertow doesn't happen for the length of the beach, it is only in certain areas. He or she will swim parallel to the beach until the outward pull declines and then with relative ease, one can make his or her way back to the shallows.

If you have never been caught in the surf and you don't know the ways of the mighty ocean, it is hard to keep your head when the current has you in its grip and you see land and safety quickly receding.

I ran to the water's edge and up to mid thigh. I knew that getting myself into trouble wouldn't help anything but I was hoping to flag down a surfer on a boogie board to help with the rescue. It felt like dejá vu.

Just two years earlier, we had been at this very same stretch of sand on a day when there was an undertow. We had been enjoying a bit of time off with the participants from one of the groups we were leading. The waves were great for jumping and body surfing, fat swells that crashed and rolled. We played like seals, cavorting in the water as many had not done since they were children. We had one woman with us, Mary Jane, who although a seasoned beach goer, underestimated the pull of the sea. Mary Jane was in her 80s and her strength just wasn't what it used to be. We quickly swam out to make sure she wasn't in danger and I found someone to loan us a boogie board on which she could float, as she kicked and Shya towed her back to shore. About that time I realized that I was moving outward and I best be attentive to the current myself. One of the other participants, Bill, was swimming in my direction, too. Bill is a large man, almost twice my weight and as I pulled along side him he was beginning to tire. "Save me!" he said.

Bill actually had plenty of strength left. It was just that the surprising power of the water had whipped him mentally.

"Bill, open your eyes and look at me," I said, "I can't save you. You are twice my size. You have to save yourself. Swim! I will swim with you and we will make it together."

Side-by-side we paddled. To look at us you would have thought we were having a leisurely conversation and a relaxing swim, as I was facing Bill side-stroking while he was on his back kicking his feet as we headed for shore. We made it to the water's edge safely that day but it was a lesson learned about the power of the sea.

Two years later, I once again tried to get a boogie boarder to loan us a board as we had done for Mary Jane, knowing that it was easier to float someone in rather than swim with him. But it seemed that other people at the beach were oblivious to the drama playing out before them. I watched and waited and eventually Shya, with his arm around the stranger's chest, towed him to shore.

The man was lean with long brown hair, straggly-looking and dazed as he stood on shaky legs. He was from Ohio, he said. He had never been to the beach before and had no idea that he could be swept to sea. Thanking Shya he staggered back to his towel and we flopped once again on ours. I had the impression that this man wouldn't be swimming in the ocean again anytime soon.

As his heartbeat calmed and the sun soothed us, Shya told me what had happened.

"I saw him bobbing and it wasn't even a thought, I knew he was in trouble. I guess all those years of saving lives hasn't left me," he said with a grin. "I got there just in time because he was slipping under the water and was only half conscious. It's a good thing he had such long hair because I grabbed a handful and hauled him back to the surface. I held him in a swimmer's 'cross-chest carry' to keep his face out of the water and help him float but the pull of the current was pretty strong. He wanted to quit. He had already let go of life, he was so exhausted and he was prepared to let me swim him in. But I couldn't. I knew I couldn't. So I told him – Kick! Kick your legs! I know you're tired, but if you don't, I'll have to let you drown. I can't do it alone. I can't save you. I can only assist. You're going to have to save yourself. – His attempts were feeble at first but it was enough. I kept encouraging him and together we made it. It reminded me, Ariel, of you helping Bill two years ago."

As we lay there on our towels, and the cloud crept over to give us shade, I thought about how perfect a day it was. Sometimes people come to us in our groups looking for us to "save" them. They are tired of doing it on their own, beaten and exhausted by bucking the currents in their lives. When someone reaches out to them, the automatic reaction is to let go and let someone else take over. But only by working as a team do we stand on safe ground once again. By working together people can discover reserves of energy they never knew existed and they can realize how capable they are.

There is nothing wrong with getting assistance if you are in over your head and you are unable to make it on your own. But you still need to swim also – to kick your feet and move your arms and really, truly save yourself.

JEWELS

As told by Shya

Several years ago we lived in Woodstock, New York where one of our favorite pastimes was to visit a store that had a very eclectic bent, as did its owner. The store's name is, "Just Joe" and Joe is a sweet, bearded man who has a passion for quality items. We bought our wedding and engagement rings from him because he carries fine jewelry. We would haunt his store on Saturday mornings because Joe made a wicked double espresso, which went well with his fine Belgian dark chocolates. We would visit on rainy days for the homemade soup du jour and just about any time to look at his antique cars, fantastic bird feeders, oriental porcelain cups and plates, hand woven shawls, kites and high quality cigars from the Canary Islands.

Joe also offered exotic, hand raised tropical birds, parrots and cockatoos. In the midst of the plethora of fun things to look at, touch and buy, stood an enormous wrought iron, handmade birdcage. This palatial cage was inhabited by Jewels, a large white, sulfur crested cockatoo from the parrot family. Jewels and I had a special relationship. Whenever I entered the store, he would stick his head out of the cage calling to me and raising his crest. The ritual was, as I approached, Jewels would arch his neck and point his head toward the floor, requesting me to work my fingers between his feathers and give his neck a scratch. When my interest faded for scratching his neck, like a dog, he would gently nibble my fingers with his beak and bump my hand with his crest, stretching even further between the bars of his cage, encouraging me to continue. This went on for several years.

Sometimes when we visited, Jewels would be out of his cage sitting on the counter or riding around on Joe's shoulder. On those occasions, Jewels greeted me and hopped over to my shoulder or hand and extended his neck to be scratched.

One afternoon, Ariel and I visited Joe's and Jewels began his customary straining against the bars of his cage, requesting attention. I said, "Would it be OK if I take Jewels out of his cage?" Joe said, "Sure, go ahead." I scratched Jewels neck in greeting and then I released the latch and pulled open the door. When I reached in and offered him my hand as a perch he did not immediately climb aboard so I nudged his feet with my fingers in hopes of encouraging him to come out and play.

In a flash, Jewels attacked the skin between my thumb and forefinger with his beak. Shocked and bleeding, I yelped and yanked my hand out of the cage. Jewels was still attached. I shook my hand until he fell free and fluttered to the floor. He then proceeded to attack my shoes. I retreated and Jewels began chasing me around the store. Joe called out, "Don't let him catch you. His beak is capable of crushing nuts and can easily pierce your shoe and break your toe."

My relationship with Jewels changed forever in that moment and was never the same thereafter. I realized that for all of Jewels' straining against the bars of his cage, he was indeed at home and felt safe there. It was his comfort zone and I had no right to reach in and try to take him out.

This interaction taught us a valuable lesson, which has supported Ariel and me in our work. If people truly want to free themselves from the confining nature of self-defeating habits, negative personal history and the story of their lives, we can assist them in doing that. If, however, people say they want to be free of the limitations that have followed them through life but are actually comfortable in their cages and are unwilling to give that up, then reaching in to take them out becomes a violent act. They will fight to defend their right to stay immersed in the reasons for their inability to be happy, healthy and live in a state of well-being.

I don't mean to give the impression that you shouldn't be willing to give someone a helping hand. What I am suggesting is that sometimes people say they want help but really don't. Ariel and I have learned to respect a person's right to stay in his or her cage. It has been our experience that if we exercise patience and keep pointing to the door, then any individual who truly wants to be free will find his or her own way out.

BUY A TICKET

Our assistant, Christina, came to work in our office one Saturday and we noticed that she seemed subdued. She didn't look like her beautiful, lively self and so we sat down with her over a cup of coffee and asked if everything was all right. Christina began to cry and through the sniffles and tears we sorted out what seemed to be the crux of the matter. She was feeling lonely and wanted a boyfriend, someone with whom she could spend time, someone who would love her and touch her and be there and yes, someone whom she could fall in love with – someone she could marry.

Over the course of the conversation, it became apparent that after her last relationship had dissolved she was so disappointed that she had retreated into herself. Even though she was the one to end things with her previous boyfriend, after the initial burst of energy that came from being honest and telling the truth, she felt drained, sad and unattractive.

We told her a story:

There once was a man who wanted so badly to win the Lotto that he complained to God on a daily basis. His complaint went something like this: "Oh, God! Why won't you let me win the Lotto? Do you hate me? I really need that money and if you were a kind God, you would have me win. If you were a fair God, surely you would support me. If you were a just God, you would make sure I got the winning numbers. Please God, let it be today."

Every day the man would watch television to see the Lotto results. Then he'd say, "God, dear God, why didn't you let me win?"

Every day the man's routine was the same. He would come home from work, turn on the TV and check the Lotto results. Every day the results were the same, he didn't win. And every day the man complained to God, that He must hate him because he didn't get the money that he so justly deserved.

One night, after going through his ritual of watching the Lotto results, from the comfort of his recliner, this poor fellow once again began his lament.

"Oh God, Oh God, why?"

Suddenly a voice came to him pleading for help. It was large and booming and seemed to emanate from all directions at once. Thinking someone was behind him the man quickly looked behind his chair but no one was there.

"Help Me!" the voice boomed again. He jumped out of his LazyBoy and frantically looked around the room for the person who was calling for help but he couldn't locate the source.

Finally, the man realized the voice must be coming from heaven. Thinking that his prayers had finally been heard he fell to his knees, sure that now with divine intervention all of his prayers would be answered.

Once again, the voice boomed out, reverberating through the house. "Help Me!" the voice entreated, "Help Me! Please, give Me a hand... Buy a ticket!"

"Christina," we said, "If you want to win the lottery, you need to buy a ticket. If you want to catch a bus, you don't stand in the woods. If you want to get a date, you can't sit at home and expect someone who has never met you to call." We told her that if she wanted to find a boyfriend, as simple as this may sound, she needed to take the actions to make it happen.

Christina was heartened by the conversation. That night she began to buy her own ticket by joining an online dating service. When she was out, she actually looked around at the available men in her environment rather than hiding behind her eyes, a smile masking her disappointment and feelings of undesirability.

One thing led to another and Christina started to participate in her own life. She decided to train for a marathon to raise money for cancer research. During training and other marathon activities Christina realized that she was surrounded by men, many of them available. But she didn't have dates. We suggested to her that she practice flirting by giving a smile here and there and staying present for the response. In fact, we suggested that she flirt everywhere, that she stay interested and engaged and talk to people whether it was in line at the bank or to the postal agent or the person who was serving her a coffee at Starbucks. It didn't matter if the person was male or female. It wasn't about getting married, just like when you buy a lottery ticket you don't expect to win the whole pot each time. The important thing was playing the game. Her chances improved each time she "bought a ticket."

Christina has been dating now. She hasn't found the man of her dreams yet but if she keeps investing, she has a much better chance than someone who plays Lotto. If you want to have a chance at your dreams, you can't just sit on the LazyBoy of life and expect that God will intervene. You need to buy your own ticket and play the game.

FOLLOWING YOUR HEART

People are driven. It is one of the strengths and failings of humanity. We are determined to accomplish, achieve or acquire what we believe to be necessary for our survival and our advancement. This driven quality creates a myopic point of view of life.

Getting ahead or being driven by an agenda can blind us to our truth, our hearts and possibilities outside of that which we rationally, reasonably can conceive.

There is a whole other way of being that most of us have not been taught growing up, yet it exists full-blown in this very moment. While one of humanity's strongest tools for survival has been its intellect and rational, reasonable mind, there is an equally potent facility available to us that we may not use as frequently – our intuition or our *heart*.

In today's world, depending on intellect is akin to being exclusively right-handed. Whenever you reach for something, you habitually do it with your right hand. It is not that you couldn't use your left but you don't even think to use it. You simply rely upon your right when, with practice, you could be equally skilled with both.

In the next chapters, we open a window into the world of your intuition, your natural knowing and following your heart. As you discover how to trust your own "left hand," you will see how unimaginable and profound moments are simply waiting to be experienced.

THAT SMALL NOT SO STILL VOICE

This chapter is devoted to hearing that small still voice; the one that normally does not insist that you listen to it, rather it comes with valuable information that you often realize was important in retrospect. It usually comes, unformed, as an impression, a flash, or a fleeting thought. Then later you say to yourself, "Oh, that's what it meant. I knew I should have..." This voice is different from the loud internal radio station, WKRAP, that plays those oldies and not so goodies, the records of how you can't or aren't good enough – the records you would eagerly smash if you got the chance.

In the following story, our friend Ty is presented with an undeniable opportunity to really listen to himself. Persistent by nature, Ty's intuition was also persistent to get him to finally take action, even though he did not believe in "that sort of thing."

Ty, a down to earth fellow in his mid-forties, has apple pink cheeks and the blush of youth. A farmer by trade, he spends his days tending his animals, preparing feed, managing workers, repairing machinery and basically keeping the farm running day-to-day. He once told us with a rueful grin that his animals would all have to up and die in order for him to take a proper vacation... we guess this is actually true.

Ty went to school and earned a degree in business and finance but chose to go back to the farm, like his father before him. As an only child, he has taken over running things on the family farm in Boring, Oregon. People might underestimate him because he is so humble, with a ready laugh and genuine interest in things, allowing him to ask questions in a guileless manner that others might find embarrassing. But if you were to sit down one day and have a casual chat with Ty, you would see the genius that is quietly sitting behind his kind eyes and his soft features.

As a man with dirt beneath his nails, Ty would be the first to tell you that he doesn't think of himself as particularly intuitive, unless it's the type of intuition that comes from years of experience – such as how to vary the feed or which antibiotic to use when his animals are showing signs of illness. So you can imagine his surprise when one frosty October evening he had a very peculiar dream. While he was sleeping, a voice came to him and very clearly said, "Return the trains."

Watching his wife softly breathing beside him, Ty thought, *That's odd. What could this mean?* It was such a specific instruction and it seemed so clear in its intent. But, he didn't understand it.

At work that morning the words, "Return the trains," came back to him so he tried to guess the meaning. But as he became involved in the long hours and heavy work, he put it out of his mind until a few days later, when the dream came again. It was just as specific and equally as frustratingly vague. "Return the trains," it commanded. Awakened in the pre-dawn hours, he lay in his bed and pondered the meaning.

Ty realized that the theme of trains, in general, did have meaning for him. He'd had a fascination for trains as long as he could remember, starting when his grandfather gave him model trains. He had adored them as a child and still cherished them as an adult. *How can I return these trains?* Ty wondered. His grandfather was long since dead.

Ty also likes real trains. When he was just a boy his grandfather took him to the train yard. With his small hand clutched in his granddad's enormous one, they would watch the trains pull in and unload grain and timber. The hoot of a night train's whistle still brought a nostalgic pang to his belly and occasionally a fluttering in his chest. But these trains were long gone; just phantoms of memory that could not be returned.

Being a practical sort, Ty dismissed the voice in his dreams and went to work. There was plenty to keep him occupied and at night, after spending the evening with his wife, he gratefully sank into bed. But sometime during the night, the voice came again. "Return the trains," it insisted.

Now this was getting annoying and kind of weird. Keeping the nocturnal auditory visits private, he wondered what it could mean. It was then that Ty remembered his Uncle Clyde and his cousin, Clyde's son Jack, who had also collected trains when he was a boy. Jack, now in his late 50's, had also been an only child. When Ty was young, his cousin, ten years older than he, sometimes babysat him and they would play trains together. But that was a lifetime ago, before Uncle Clyde died from a brain tumor.

Early in the morning, Ty ruminated on the last time he saw his uncle alive. It was in 1984 when Uncle Clyde was close to death and in hospice care. He had visited him in the upstairs of Clyde's old home. Even though his breathing was labored and his face was pale, his uncle was glad to see him. Ty was glad he had made the effort to go. The families were not particularly close. There had been no major falling out – it was just the way his folks were. Ty had not seen Jack for several years. When he came in, Jack was at his father's bedside. A full Colonel in the Green Berets, he looked fierce in his lace up black boots and military uniform. Ty was impressed with the powerful man he had become.

"What are you doing here?" Jack had snapped. "Get out of this house. I never want to lay eyes on you again!"

Jack had looked like he meant it and that he had the means to back up the implied threat in his words. So, apart from the funeral a few days later, Ty had not seen his cousin in nearly two decades.

Suddenly Ty remembered one train in his extensive collection that he had not bought and neither had his grandfather. There was one Lionel in mint condition, still in its box, that had once belonged to Jack. When Ty was 13 and Jack was 23, his Uncle Clyde had deemed that Jack was too old for toys and had carelessly given the train to Ty and never thought of it again.

As Ty lay in his bed that night, he realized that yes, there was one train he could return. In the light of day, however, the farm demanded that he get to his chores so he put it out of his mind.

It seems that the mysterious voice had other ideas. It intruded on his sleep now every night, getting more specific. "Return the trains," it commanded, "by Christmas!"

Thinking back on it later, Ty realized that he was a little cranky during that time, from having broken sleep. It was almost like having a young child in the house who didn't care whether or not Ty needed sleep or if he was dead tired from a hard day. The voice called out to get his attention and to spur him to action. But Ty was dragging his feet. He didn't believe in supernatural phenomena, you see. He believed in practicalities: animal husbandry, the earth, the seasons and such. So he put up with the noise and lack of sleep and went about his day with the kind of stubborn determination that helps a farmer make it though lean seasons.

New Year's came and went as winter turned the corner and headed into spring. But the voice was not finished with Ty yet. It, too, was determined and keeping pace with the calendar, it began to wake him again. "Return the trains," it said. Now there was a new instruction. "Return the trains by Easter!"

Eventually Ty thought, *Enough is enough.* The Saturday afternoon before Easter Sunday, Ty placed the box with the little train in a brown shopping bag. He donned a red pullover, khaki pants and a pair of clean work boots and whistled to his chocolate Labrador Retriever, Hershey, to come along for moral support. As he got ready to climb into his truck, Ty was struck by a thought, *What if he doesn't recognize me?* It had been 20 years after all. Actually, Jack lived in Boring, Oregon also and it seemed slightly odd to him that their paths had never crossed in all that time.

Ty considered everything he knew about his cousin, things that had drifted down through casual familial conversations over the last 20 years. Ty knew that Jack had been willed Clyde's home and that Jack was retired from the military for a number of years. He also knew that Jack volunteered for some of the local charities and organizations, such as the Boy Scouts. Other than that, he didn't know Jack's habits or schedule. He didn't know if he was even in town. All Ty knew was that, if possible, it was time to quiet the nocturnal voice.

Ty decided to leave the truck at home and take his mint condition, 1978, persimmon colored, 280Z sports car for such an important a trip. As he backed it carefully out of the barn, he remembered that this was the car he drove the last time he saw Jack. Maybe it would spark some recognition in his cousin.

Pulling up the fir-lined drive, the house looked very much like he remembered, although maybe a bit smaller. He held the bag by the handles, told his dog to stay, and climbed out of his Z, taking in the rambling porch, the sloping lawn, the azalea bush with tight pink buds. Resolutely, Ty climbed the house steps, the slanted afternoon light leaving a long shadow in his wake. He knocked on the door, his pulse quickening as he waited. It wasn't long before the door swung open and there stood Jack, looking a little older and leaner, his military bearing showing even when wearing a t-shirt and faded blue jeans.

Jack's eyebrows lifted almost to his hairline as he blurted, "What are you doing here?" Oddly enough, it was the same thing he'd growled at Ty 20 years before, just upstairs from where they were now standing.

At this moment, Ty really didn't want to be where he was, standing on the porch in the late afternoon sun with the faint smell of pine wafting on the breeze and his dog waiting patiently for him in the Z. However, he knew this was where he had to be, for things seemed to crystallize as he thrust forward the large brown shopping bag that held the box with the little Lionel inside.

"Here," he said. "This is for you. It's yours."

Mystified, Jack looked inside the bag that glowed in the sun, the contents illuminated as effectively as if he had used a spotlight. Much to Ty's surprise, his cousin, a man close to 60 years of age, a retired Green Beret Colonel, burst into tears. It was the kind of crying that spontaneously leaps from the eye in fat drops. Jack turned away, leaned his hand on the back of a chair that stood beside the kitchen table, flung his other arm across his eyes and wept.

In that moment, Ty took a chance, a single step that meant so much. Lifting a foot in his clean work boot, he stepped over the door lintel and into the kitchen. His cousin's earlier angry words, "What are you doing here? Get out of this house. I never want to lay eyes on you again!" had implied a threat of physical harm. Now it was wiped away and 20 years of separation ended with that one simple move.

Collecting himself, Jack pulled out the chair he'd been leaning against. He motioned to Ty to sit and pulled over one for himself.

Quietly closing the door, Ty sat and waited.

Jack said, "I'm sorry! I'm sorry for the mean things I said last time I saw you. I never meant it, really. I was just in such pain and my father had been so distant to me. I could never do it right enough or well enough; it seemed he favored you. Please forgive me. I cut you out of my life and it wasn't your fault. I was just in pain."

Ty's rosy cheeks became rosier. Never in his wildest dreams had he expected this kind of reaction or reception. All he wanted to do was stop that damn voice. But this wasn't the biggest surprise. He was about to be shocked again. Over two mugs of steaming coffee, Jack made another confession:

"Ty, this is going to sound strange, but I've been having these dreams. Each night a voice would come to me and I couldn't imagine what it meant, but now I know. The voice kept repeating the same thing over and over. It said, 'The trains are coming!'"

These two grown and very practical men looked at each other sheepishly as Ty explained his dreams instructing him to return the trains. Neither of them believed in ghosts or phantoms or wee beasties that go bump in the night. They both believed in the sun coming up in the morning and going down in the evening and the good hard work that came in between. But believe it or not, the small, not so still voice had led them back to one another; back to being family and friends.

Perhaps Ty's experience will give you an added push to reach out and take those challenging actions of your own, even if you don't have proof that this is the "right" thing to do. Sometimes a hunch is the best information you are going to get. When you act upon your intuition, you just may find that that small, not so still voice has your best interests at heart.

DISCOVERING YOUR TRUE HEART'S DESIRE

As told by Ariel

When Shya and I went to Bali, Indonesia for the first time as speakers for an Earth Conference, we met Oka one day, seemingly by chance. Our tour bus had stopped at the residence of a famous mask sculptor in the little woodcarving village of Mas. Shya and I tired of the exhibit long before our fellow travelers did and we elected to wander next door to kill some time and see what the neighboring shop had to offer. What started out to be a pleasant afternoon's diversion radically altered the shape of our lives.

On our way to the inner recesses of the adjacent gallery, we were captured by the sight of figures in a small glass case, exquisite little carvings made from sandalwood. As we opened the glass door the pungent aroma of the wood wafted out to greet us. Shya picked up a small, perfect, serene carving of a Buddha head. Its features seemed quiet and alive – almost as if the Buddha could open his eyes and speak to us. As Shya held the figurine, a young man who had been leaning against the wall said quietly, "Oh, please, if you buy him, do not keep him out in the sun. He took me almost **two** weeks to carve."

This soft-spoken fellow, dressed in a well-worn sarong and white t-shirt, was I.B. Oka, a twelfth-generation woodcarver. Oka descended from a long line of Hindu priests and white magicians, but we didn't know that at the time. All we knew was this fascinating fellow with a full head of jet-black hair looked far too young and far too unimposing in stature to have attained such mastery in wood.

There was something about Oka's work that caught my breath and moved my heart at the same time. I appreciated the simplicity of his form and style. Reluctantly and with reverence, we returned the Buddha head to its case so we could take a tour and see what other delightful finds were in other parts of the gallery. As we went through the next couple of rooms, admiring a mask here and a statue there, we found that most pieces that moved us were made by Oka himself, even though there were many artisans' works hanging on the walls.

As we continued through the gallery, soaking up the view and sipping cold water that Oka had offered, we came upon an extraordinary carving, a "Breyut." In Bali, any set of parents that has four or more children is called a Breyut. Couples who are having trouble conceiving will seek out and bring offerings to a Breyut statue, which represents fertility and fruitfulness. There, they will pray for a child. The statue before us had been carved from the root structure of a hibiscus tree. Emerging from the solid wood center out to the root tendrils were a mother, father, their firstborn and fifteen other children. The figures seemed to be resting in flowers or sprouting from flames. The children were all carved with almost no features and large spatular fingers as if they were waiting to be imprinted by the souls who were to inhabit them.

Oka stood beside us and said in a quiet voice, "Every night for over a year I carved on that piece of wood. My family thought I was crazy to spend so much time on something that would never be sold, but I had to do it. Already I have Breyuts in other villages that have helped to bring the villagers children."

I had to touch the babies' heads and trace the flames with my fingers. The surface was so smooth. For no apparent reason, I began to cry. I had heard of being moved to tears, but not since I was young had I felt the kind of inspiration that I felt being near this carving.

It was time to get back to our tour. Reluctantly, I left the inner sanctum of the gallery. Shaking Oka's hand, we thanked him for his time.

Later that night, I dreamt of the Breyut. The next morning, as I hovered between wakefulness and dreaming, I rolled on my side while visions of the Breyut floated softly past my mind's eye. I didn't realize that Shya was also awake until he said, "OK, Ariel, we'll go back and get it. I knew we would find you a birthday present here. I just never had any idea it would be a four foot tall statue."

We hired a car and drove back to Mas the next day, the Breyut drawing us like a magnet. Strolling to the back of the gallery, Shya and Oka had a conversation.

"My wife has fallen in love with one of your statues, Oka, and I hope we can afford it."

"Which one?" came the soft reply.

Shya stood in front of the masterpiece, "This one, your Breyut."

Shaking his head Oka said, "I'm sorry. It's not for sale."

My heart sank, but without missing a beat Shya looked him in the eye and said, "Well, if it was for sale, how much would it be?"

Dark intense eyes returned his gaze as if Oka were taking measure of the man before him. If we bought the Breyut, would we give these children of his inspired touch a good home, or were we simply foreign merchants looking to turn a profit by reselling his art? Eventually Oka named his price and we struck a deal.

We agreed to bring him the money in a few days when we had another break in our conference and he agreed to make a crate and pack our treasure. I was elated. As we were leaving, Oka looked at me.

"When you return, Ariel, I will have a gift for you, a tiny sandalwood Buddha this big," he said indicating the size of the tip of his index finger. "He will sit in an ebony case which looks like a closed lotus blossom. When you open the flower, the Buddha will be seated inside."

The day we returned with payment, Oka was true to his word. As he wrapped my hand around the ebony lotus, inside of which was hidden the little sandalwood fellow, his tone turned serious.

"Ariel, if you put this by your bed tonight, the Buddha will come to you in your dreams."

Yeah sure, I thought. Yet, I smiled as I thanked him for the gift so as not to cause offense.

Despite my cynical immediate response to Oka's suggestion, I was like a child with a new toy that day. I would have to wait months for my Breyut to arrive home to America, but I had a small tangible reminder of its greatness nestled in the lotus in my hand. Over and over throughout the afternoon, I opened the wooden flower to find the hidden treasure, serenely waiting for me inside.

That evening, before we went to sleep, I put the Buddha by my bedside. Soon I had a dream:
It was night and I was standing on the edge of a miniature golf course with a putter in my hand. Standing near me was a young boy with blond hair who looked up at me and said, "Come on, Ariel! Let's go putt-putt golfing."

"OK," I replied, "but you know I'm not very good at this."

Just then I heard a familiar, soft voice, "Excuse me, please, but you know that is not true. You are very good at anything you enjoy doing."

Looking up, I saw Oka. Balanced in his open palm stood the open ebony lotus and, of course, the Buddha. I knew now that I was dreaming, but the feel of the club in my hand and the bright green of the imitation grass on the putting surfaces seemed very real.

Early the next morning when I awoke, the dream remained vivid. As simple as it was, it precipitated a profound shift in me. As I lay there in the semi-darkness of our room I became aware of Shya peacefully slumbering beside me, his deep and rhythmic breaths playing background music to my musings.

The message of my dream replayed in my head, "Excuse me, but you know that's not true. You are very good at anything you enjoy doing." Different scenes from my childhood and then more recent life played like a video. Distant events sorted and reorganized themselves even as I watched.

There were activities, projects and sports. There were the endeavors I had held as failures. Other vignettes I remembered as triumphs and some fell in between. But somewhere in the midst of all these experiences, that I had always judged as successes or failures, was the truth that anything that had been inspired by my heart, expressions of my true self, I had become accomplished at. I also realized that other relationships and passions petered out not because I was no good at them, but because they were not a part of my true heart's desire.

Moments in time strung together like pearls, all leading to that instant. I felt a sense of perfection and deep relaxation. As I drifted back to sleep that morning, my face was a mirror of the miniature one sitting on my bedside table.

UPSETS

As we grow up in a family, we imitate the behaviors of the people around us. If they manipulate their life circumstances by getting upset or threatening to get upset, this is passed on from generation to generation.

Most people, even in the best of times, live from one upset to the next and frequently, these episodes overlap. They are initiated when things don't go the way we would prefer. In these circumstances, the automatic response is to get upset, as if being disturbed will somehow force the circumstances to change.

There are times when being upset is really in avoidance of handling something that is challenging. It may be a way of avoiding a communication that we don't know how to deliver or a tactic used to delay starting a new or confronting project. In truth, however, being upset does not serve us in any positive way.

In this section, we offer various views on upsets as well as successful strategies for side-stepping or extricating yourself from them. Join us and develop mastery over disturbing situations so you can return to your true self in challenging times.

APPLY THE BRAKES AND BACK OUT
As told by Shya

Sarah was sitting to our right and it was clear that she had a burning desire to speak. We were leading one of our Monday evening seminars in Manhattan and Sarah was radiating her frustration – the subject of which was yet to be revealed.

Ariel must have decided to give her a bit of help saying, "Who has a question or wants to say something?" Her gaze floated across the sea of faces and landed with a smile on Sarah.

Sarah is an African American woman in her early 40s. She has a fiery nature, offset by her natural elegance. She leapt at the chance and jumped to her feet.

"Ariel, Shya," she said, "I'm so frustrated I can hardly stand myself." She waved her hands with a dramatic and slightly humorous flourish.

With mock seriousness I asked, "What happened?" which caused Sarah to chuckle and ratcheted her tension down considerably.

"I keep getting upset! It drives me crazy. And I can't seem to help myself. I go from upset-to-upset; they keep growing like weeds!"

"Do you drive?" I asked.

"What?" Sarah looked confused. She was just about to tell us the dramatic details of her upset. But she didn't know that repeating those details could very likely restart the cycle of being upset again.

"A car. Do you know how to drive a car?"

Slowly she nodded yes. I could tell she was wondering where I was going and what it had to do with being upset.

"Well, if you were driving your car and you made a turn onto a one-way street and discovered that you were going the wrong way, what's the first thing you'd do?"

"Scream!"

The group laughed and Ariel smiled, too, as she said, "Let's assume that screaming is not necessary in this situation, OK?"

I asked again, "If you turned onto a one-way street and discovered that you were now pointing the wrong direction, what's the first thing, aside from screaming, you should do?"

"Look behind me."

"Well if you did that, then you might keep going and hit something."

"Oh, that's true," Sarah said. "I'd stop."

"Right, you'd apply the brakes and, if possible, you'd back out. Upsets are like that, Sarah. When you start to get upset, just apply the brakes and back out."

Ariel continued, "Many years ago, Shya and I rented a home and our landlord lived next door. He was a very disagreeable man and we found ourselves repeatedly upset by his behavior. One very hot summer evening, Shya and I went for a late night walk. There was no one around since we lived in the country. As we walked up the road we brought our landlord with us... in our complaints. He went up the road and down, keeping us company as we found ourselves once again upset by something that had already happened that we had no hope of changing. We were deeply in the upset and complaint compartment in our minds. This is the equivalent of driving down a one-way street in the wrong direction. Right then and there we agreed to back out of that compartment. And you know what, it worked."

Sarah looked thoughtful. This was clearly something that never had occurred to her. A slow smile spread across her face. "Really, do you think I can do that?" and then a moment later, "How do I do that?"

All of us had a good chuckle at that.

"Well, Sarah, when you're complaining, you're saying that things shouldn't be as they are, that the moment isn't perfect."

"But it isn't... just look at my hair! In all this humidity it just goes frizzy." She grinned.

"Ahh, Sarah," Ariel continued. "You hit on the key. A full blown upset is just the tip of the iceberg. If you find yourself rolling from one upset to another, start by looking at those small seemingly harmless complaints."

Sarah cocked her head to the side, "How do you mean?"

"Let's go back to the Three Principles of Transformation, shall we?" I prompted. "The first principle is: Anything you resist will persist and grow stronger. Take a small complaint. Any complaint is a form of resistance. The more you complain about your hair, for instance, the more attention you place on it. The more weight it takes on, no pun intended."

Sarah smiled, touched her hair and nodded.

"Next is the Second Principle of Transformation which states that you can only be exactly as you are in any given moment. In other words, you can only have the hair you have or be standing where you are right now and you couldn't be in any other place being any other way, really. Of course each of us has a fantasy of how things could be or perhaps should be different, but Sarah, you can only be here exactly as you are right now."

Sarah still looked a little confused, but she was relaxing. She was no longer poised on the top of the slide preparing to jump down that slippery slope into an upset.

Ariel took over from there, "Sarah, the Third Principle of Transformation is: Anything that you allow to *be,* without judging it or trying to fix it, will complete itself and cease to dominate you and your life."

"Let me explain further," I said. "If you find yourself complaining or upset, that is the only way you can be in that moment. Let's pretend that my fingers are a digital camera and as I snap my fingers I take a picture of your image. Is it possible that in that instant you could have been seated?"

"No of course not!" she said with a breathless grin. Sarah was engaged in this conversation and her upset was gone.
"Well, can you possibly be not upset when you are?"

"No," she said a bit more slowly this time. "If I am upset, that is how I am. I may have a fantasy of things getting better, but it is obvious that things are the way they are, especially when I am upset. But, I don't like it and I want to change it." She said stamping her foot.

We all had to laugh as Sarah was actually happily outlining her dilemma.

"OK, Sarah, not liking it takes you right back to the first principle: What you resist persists. Of course, if the second principle is true, as we have seen that it is, then if you don't like being upset, then you can only not like being upset, also. You can only be you, however you are, in any given moment. Luckily, there is a Third Principle of Transformation: Anything you allow to be exactly as it is will complete itself and stop dominating you."

"OK," she said, "I am beginning to see."

"Your earlier solution about screaming when you see that you are going down a one-way street in the wrong direction was more than just a good joke, it is really how you approach these upsets. When you find yourself upset, you complain and scream in your thoughts. You don't realize that you can simply skip that step. It is possible that you can just stop, literally apply the brakes and back out of that compartment."

At this point our friend, Andy, who was sitting to our left stood up and asked, "May I add something?"

"Of course, Andy." Ariel said.

"Sarah, I have a little boy, Alex. He is four-years-old and he had a temper tantrum the other day because he didn't want to brush his teeth. He was mad at me and said that he didn't understand why I got to make all of the rules. He wanted to make some rules. I calmly told him that brushing his teeth wasn't my rule it was the Doctor's rule. After Alex brushed his teeth, I sat on the floor with him and we talked. I talked about this upset he had been experiencing. 'Alex,' I said, 'do you know that feeling you get when you are upset, how it comes over you?' He nodded yes, so I said, 'Well then if you want to make a rule, if you want to be in charge, you can tell it no! Tell it to go away.' Alex looked thoughtful and then his whole face lit up and he shouted, 'I can tell it to go to jail!'"

We all laughed as Andy finished his tale. "This was a four-year-old's funny version of saying "no," of applying the brakes and backing out of going down a one-way street in the wrong direction. I have watched him wrestle with the feelings since then. Sometimes he even shouts out loud and we laugh as he learns that he is in charge, not the upset."

There was a smattering of applause and Sarah was smiling as she and Andy both sat back down. From her chair she piped up, "I guess I can learn a thing or two from a four-year-old! Thank you, Andy. Thank you, Ariel and Shya. I am excited to see what happens from here."

"Are you upset now?" I asked.

Sarah sat up a little straighter in her chair as she replied, "Not at all. My car is traveling in the right direction and I am at the wheel."

STARTING OVER

Have you ever found yourself in one of those moods where no matter what your partner says or does, it's fodder for a fight? You know how it feels when you're so angry and disturbed and nothing he or she says or does is good enough to relieve your sense of aggravation?

We recently met a couple who were in one of these altered states of consciousness. They came to speak to us about their relationship and how, no matter what they did, it always ended in an upset and distress. The fight never seemed to completely resolve. Oh sure, it abated from time-to-time, but the embers of disagreement were always just below a thin skin, ready to erupt at any time.

The funny thing about it was they were both right, from their individual points-of-view. From his point-of-view, "She would always..." and from her point of view, he was wrong and all of her friends agreed with her take on the situation. This couple had a list of grievances that dated back very early in their relationship, past events over which the two of them continued to disagree.

Hal and Mary were stuck in the same fundamental behavior patterns that we have seen in other intimate relationships where nothing seems to resolve. No matter how much they tried to change or fix the situation, it stayed the same or became worse.

They came to us, looking at whether or not they should remain together. Their situation was further complicated by the fact that they had a 16-month-old child together. By now, the sense of intimacy between the two of them had completely eroded and while they were very devoted to their daughter, she had become the focal point for many of their fights.

The real problem was that Mary and Hal, for all of their strife, were obviously still in love. They just couldn't find a way to sidestep the old grievances that kept resurfacing, incendiary mechanical behaviors, that set them battling against their will.

Our usual approach is to find out where it all started and what happened that initiated the fight. When we asked what caused this pattern of behavior in the first place, Hal and Mary each had their reasons for what the other did or didn't do that created the situation and both of them were "right" from their points-of-view. Apparently, we had a stalemate. No matter what we came up with, each person felt certain that the other was the cause of their stress, upset and dissatisfaction. This is normal for most relationships that are in trouble.

In situations like the one with Hal and Mary, in which they have been together several years, the starting point of the disagreement is obscured forever. So what do you do to alleviate the pain when you're locked in a habitual way of relating that seems to have no beginning and no end? A way of relating that keeps accelerating in its frequency, intensity, and duration?

At some point, the reasons why you are upset become irrelevant because everything becomes grounds for the disturbance. It has been unresolved for so long, there is no way to go back and fix all of the grievances and transgressions.

So what do you do? You can leave each other, which is the end result that a lot of loving relationships devolve into... it is called divorce. You can punish each other perpetually and live a life of complaint and pain. Or, you can start over.

There have been times in our relationship when we have found ourselves fighting and we could not find a way out of the disagreement. Finally, we came up with a device that allowed us to stop fighting. This is what happened: One day, we were driving into New York City and we were deeply engaged in disagreeing with each other. It escalated and it was like a sore tooth that you worry with your tongue; we couldn't seem to leave it alone. Our silences were noisy, very noisy. And, each of us was certain that we were right in our own perspective and that the other was simply wrong. We each felt picked on and misunderstood. It didn't feel good, but there didn't seem to be a way to resolve the conflict.

Finally, we came up with the idea of starting over. We picked an overpass ahead on the highway and said, "When we go under that overpass, it's over." This meant that as soon as our car passed that spot we were going to operate as if this disagreeable conversation had never taken place. Onward we drove. It took discipline at first to resist the temptation of thinking about the altercation that had just happened but we kept bringing our thoughts and conversation to current things such as what we could see out of the window and our plans for the day rather than rehashing the past.

We can't remember now what our fight was about. It seemed so important at the time, but now the details have faded into obscurity. We knew that the fight could fade away for Hal and Mary too, if given a chance, so we suggested to them to try starting over. We warned them it would be challenging to not keep going back to past gripes but they grew excited and intrigued at the idea.

That night, Hal and Mary had a date. They had not been on a real, live date since before their child was born.

The point in time where Hal and Mary started over was the opportunity for a new beginning. They grabbed onto this chance with both hands and intimacy resulted. However, the next time an upsetting event happened between the two of them or a similar type of disagreement cropped up over their child, it took discipline to resist the temptation to revisit old events. With practice, the habit of going back to touch on old events in your thoughts or in your actions can fade away.

THE ACCIDENTAL GIFT

As told by Shya

The night was dark, the roads unfamiliar, and we were darn tired when we pulled into a small fishing village one Halloween. It was the beginning of a short vacation, and an adventure that was to teach us a few lessons, specifically about towing a boat, and in general, about life.

Ariel and I had loaded our 22-foot boat on the trailer, hitched it to our Chevy Suburban and set out, maps in hand, on the 12-hour drive to Harker's Island, North Carolina. I must admit, it was a little daunting to be hauling three tons of fiberglass and engine, especially when we reached a traffic light or had to make any kind of sudden stop. Our momentum and the weight of the boat would continue to push us forward even after we applied the brakes. I had become accustomed to anticipating and compensating for the load, but there were times when the nose of our SUV encroached on an intersection more than we would have liked.

The trip was long and tiring, and when we finally reached our destination, night had fallen. We had to look for the rental house with only a vague idea of how the neighborhood was laid out. Ariel spotted our vacation home just as we were passing its driveway, so I needed to find a good spot to turn around.

Witches and fairies, ninjas and pirates, all kept emerging from the blackness so I needed to be extra careful to not inadvertently hit one of the young trick-or-treaters who were ghosting all around us. About this time, I made my big "mistake" by pulling into a narrow tree-shrouded lane and attempting to back up, turning sharply, to reverse direction.

When backing up with a trailer in tow, it is important that the trailer doesn't turn at an angle greater than 90 degrees. If this happens, the trailer tow hitch will hit the back bumper, doing damage to both. Unfortunately, I did just that. Before we knew it was happening, the trailer bent where it attached to our tow ball. Now, the trailer had no brakes at all because the accident had totally broken the actuator. (This is the mechanism that engages the trailer's hydraulic brake system.) Eventually, I managed to turn around without any further mishap and carefully made it back to where we would be staying.

The next morning, in the light of day, I realized that our trailer was as twisted as we had feared. This was the perfect opportunity to either get upset or do something about it. Ariel and I decided to skip the upset and get on with our day. Once we launched the boat and secured it at the marina, we spent the beginning of our vacation hunting for a trailer repair shop that could mend the damage.

As luck would have it, there was a company specializing in just that a few miles away. However, the exact part we needed was out of stock, so they suggested replacing it with something similar. After being reassured that the new part would work as well as the old (before we damaged it), we left our trailer and went fishing.

A few days later, when we received the call to pick up our trailer, we were in for quite a surprise. On first inspection, the unit looked quite different, but it seemed okay. However, when we went to attach it to the tow-ball, we weren't prepared for what happened next.

Traditionally, attaching our trailer required finesse, a bit of pushing and pulling, sweat, and occasionally a good jolt with the heel of a shoe. Now, a simple lift of a lever, and as I cranked the trailer down I heard a sweet sound, kachink, as it dropped effortlessly in place. This was hard to believe so Ariel took over and did it again and... kachink! Very pleased with this turn of events, we paid for the repair, hooked up the trailer, and left the lot. And guess what, we now had brakes... really had brakes. Suddenly, when the brake pedal was depressed, the brakes on the trailer worked, too. That was the moment we realized that our original unit had never, really worked. Grinning, both Ariel and I looked forward to the upcoming stop sign and the next traffic signal. No longer were we being pushed from behind, even when we carried the full weight of the boat.

Because this was the first time Ariel or I had ever towed something large, we didn't realize that it wasn't working correctly because we had nothing to compare it with. We assumed that the difficulties we were experiencing were normal; just a part of towing a boat. So, we learned to compensate, making the best of what we had. Then, by accident – literally – we discovered that things could be far easier and better than we had imagined.

When the two of us returned to work and started consulting clients on both personal topics and business matters, our trailer mishap provided a valuable metaphor. There are things that people put up with, in relationships, at work, and at home because they have no experience, no clue that there is another possibility. Since an individual's reality is determined by what he or she already knows, when something doesn't fit preconceived ideas, people get frustrated, upset and disturbed. Most people don't realize that the universe provides us with everything we need in each moment to have a miraculous life. Had the trailer not broken, we would have continued to struggle with it. Towing a boat was frustrating and nerve-wracking, but we didn't know it could get any better.

Sometimes the greatest gifts are those things that you come upon by accident. The next time something goes "wrong," look for the gift in it. You may just be pleasantly surprised.

POOR LITTLE DEER
As told by Ariel

My friend Isabelle is a sweet and compassionate person. She has the gift of empathy for others, which can be challenging for her as she feels so deeply. Shya and I have often tried to show her that the situations she finds distressing aren't necessarily causing her the discomfort she often feels. We have suggested that circumstances don't cause her emotions since she is perfectly capable of generating sadness, fear and pain all on her own.

I once told her about the time my sisters, Cathy, Mary and I were home alone and bored one Saturday afternoon when we were children. Somehow the conversation came around to burglars and boogiemen. Perhaps it was because we had just returned from riding our bikes past the "hillbilly's" house which was set back off the road behind a thicket of wild blackberry bushes. He was reputed to catch little girls and cook their hair for sauerkraut. I had never seen anyone come or go from this ramshackle home but I believed the story with all my heart and never failed to pedal as fast as my little legs would go when we rode past the property. Whatever the reason, it occurred to one of us that we were alone that day without an adult to protect us. Then we decided that because we were in the country, if anyone tried to break into the house or to hurt us, we could scream and no one would hear. We chewed on this topic for a while until one of us had the bright idea to test our theory.

Three young girls can sure make a big racket when they put their minds to it. And they make even more of a fuss when they get caught up in being terrified, even if it is self-induced. Once we began screaming, the dog began frantically barking and we scared ourselves silly. Before the afternoon was over, we had run around the house securing and re-securing all of the windows and doors. We brought the dog in for comfort and sat huddled on the couch under a blanket.

When Shya and I talked to Isabelle about self-induced emotions, she understood the concept but it still was rather vague, until she had a real life experience of her own.

One day at dusk, I drove Isabelle to the local fruit stand to get some sweet, ripe peaches. Since Shya and I live in the country where there are still farms, woods and fields, there is an abundance of deer in our area. It is not unusual to see a deer along the side of the road that has been struck and killed by a motorist.

As I made a turn onto the lane next to the farm stand, Isabelle caught sight of just such a dead animal. "Oh the poor little deer!" she cried. "I hope it didn't suffer. Oh, it's so sad." I could see her upset building as her hand flew to her mouth to hold in the emotion evoked by the death of this poor creature. I looked at her in surprise. Yes, it was unfortunate that a deer had been killed. The thought flitted through my mind that the person who hit it was probably upset, too, if their car was badly dented. I thought that Isabelle's response was exaggerated for the situation but I did my best to be respectful of her sadness... until I looked more closely at the deer.

I laughed. Stricken, Isabelle quickly looked at me as if to say, *How could you be so callous and cruel?*

Gliding the car to a stop, I pulled over. "I'm sorry Isabelle. I don't mean to make fun of you but please, take another look."

The poor little deer was, in fact, a brown colored rock. Isabelle had taken this sentimental journey into sadness and emotion by mistaking a rock beside the road for a poor little deer.

We still chuckle about it to this day. If she begins to get herself worked up over something and it begins to look dramatic or sad or take on epic proportions, we just look at one another and say, "Oh, the poor little deer!" That's our cue to step back from the drama and look again at the situation with clearer eyes and an unsentimental head.

Yes, Isabelle has had events in her life since then that have authentically been filled with loss, ripe with emotion such as the death of a family member. Her awareness, though, has helped her see that she has a predisposition towards drama and upset for its own sake. By seeing this, and not making herself wrong for the habit, Isabelle has been able to let go of those day-to-day "traumas" so that her life is not an endless rollercoaster of ups and downs. Yes, those "poor little deer" now honestly have no more emotional weight than a brown colored rock.

ENGAGING IN LIFE

Satisfaction comes from *Being Here* in this present moment. But since most of us have not discovered how to access the moment, true satisfaction remains elusive. What if the simple act of engaging in your life could transform it from an ordinary existence into a deeply satisfying one? What if the act of engaging is enough to bring forth your potential and allow your life to be truly fulfilling?

Join us as we explore how to engage in life, not only by bringing yourself up to speed, but also, when necessary, by slowing down.

THE PICTURE WINDOW OF YOUR LIFE
As told by Shya

Swinging my legs over the side of the bed, I grimaced at the throbbing in my right knee. It had been just two days since I had arthroscopic knee surgery to repair torn cartilage and I was still swollen, sore and dopey from the pain medication. Yet I was determined to make my way to the kitchen where I heard Ariel preparing food.

I slowly hobbled down the hall and into the kitchen and there she was, chopping carrots for her homemade chicken soup. As I rounded the corner, I saw the orange of the carrots, the flash of the knife and Ariel's face lifting and brightening when she saw me. Hands on both sides of my face; a quick lovely kiss; and she disappeared only to return moments later with a chair for me to sit near her while she worked.

Normally accustomed to being very active, my leg had laid me low and I was thrust by circumstance into a restful posture. Slightly detached, yet itching to do more, I said, "You don't mind if I just sit here do you?" I knew the answer. After all, she had just brought me the chair. But I had to ask.

"Don't be silly!" she replied. "I love your company."

And so I sat. I admired the multitude of subtle colors on our slate floor, the richness of the cherry and walnut cabinets and my wife, who was happily making us a meal, content with my quiet presence. Then my attention shifted to the big picture window over the sink with a view of the backyard. From there you can see the two hydrangea trees on either side of our lawn, weighted down with large blooms that go papery-dry in the fall and become snow laden in winter. Ariel once captured a photograph of a bright red cardinal as it perched, a crimson splash amidst the white snow crested blossoms. It was so stunning in contrast that we have made holiday cards featuring the image.

Behind the lawn are woods with oak, maple and beech trees. The leaves were beginning to turn. Mostly yellow and brown so far; not much red yet. The ferns on the edge of the forest were yellowing also, but still mainly green. Just beyond our deck is a very large freestanding bird feeder. When Ariel and I first purchased it, we still lived in Woodstock, New York. When we brought it home, the birds were afraid of it. We used to laugh because it was such an investment and we rarely attracted any takers for the feed. At that time, it was our "lawn ornament."

However, now that we live in New Jersey, the birds love this feeder for whatever reason. But then again, so do bears. I was forced to reconstruct it on three separate occasions after it was ripped apart by local black bears and I don't think it could survive a fourth attack. Now we have a little electric fence running around it, just enough to act as a deterrent, we hope. No new feeder raids since I installed the fence.

As I sat in my chair, most of this view was from memory. Sitting as I was, a distance from the window itself, I only saw an abbreviated view. From there, I could not see the lawn. Nor could I catch a glimpse of the hydrangea trees, the porch railing, the bird feeder stand or the surrounding electric fence. The tops of the trees were nipped off and so were the base of the trunks and the ferns that surrounded them.

Such is the way when you sit back, disengaged from your life. Of course, in my circumstantially enforced meditative pose, it was entirely appropriate for me to be at a distance, but it triggered a thought about the folks we coach. There are many things that can rock people back on their heels so that they are no longer up against the picture window of life – disappointment, loss, indecision. In fact, when making a life decision, people often step back, disengage and think about what to do. But from this posture, there are no treetops, no ground cover, and the edges of what is available is obscured from view.

I remembered a young man, Steven, who came to our seminars. He seemed very bright but lacked direction, focus and motivation. Unemployed for some time, his wife supported them both while he sat back and pondered what to do with his life. But no matter where he looked, he considered everything, all manner of work, as beneath him. I suggested that he stop worrying about the "right" or the "prestigious" job, and that he just get any job, even if it was making french fries at McDonald's. (After all he was from France.) I also suggested that he go about his work as if it mattered. "Do everything with excellence," I encouraged.

The next week, Steven actually found a job at the local McDonald's. Very quickly, he became the fastest, best person who had ever made french fries for the lunch rush and they offered to make him a manager. By this time, Steven had also taken a second job at Barnes & Noble. He went about this job with excellence, too, and he was soon offered a full-time job as a department manager there, as well. Now Steven was coming up to speed, moving closer to the picture window of his life.

Steven accepted the full-time managerial position at the bookstore. Before he knew it, his life was no longer a lethargic mental exercise of *What do I want to do with my life?* It became a game of looking and seeing what else was possible. With his wife's support, Steven decided to go back to school. He enrolled in a local college and the folks at the bookstore valued him as a person and as an employee so they arranged his schedule around his classes. Semester after semester, Steven earned straight A's as he took classes in advanced math and molecular biology. He would come to our weekly evening seminars excitedly talking about the day's lab experiments.

We haven't seen Steven in some years, but I hear he has his PhD and has become the head of a research lab at a prestigious university. Here is a man who took control of his life by engaging in it, with totality. He pressed his nose up against the picture window and went with what he saw without worrying about doing the "right" thing or the "better" thing.

I brought my attention back to the kitchen and realized I had sat long enough. It was time to nap again. I hoisted myself from my chair, kissed my wife, munched a piece of carrot and returned to my bed. But not before I leaned close to the window, looking far and wide.

SLOWING DOWN
As told by Ariel

It was a cold sunny day in New Jersey and the first thin layers of ice were forming on our pond. We were scheduled to go to Pilates that day, our private exercise class with a trainer, but we liked doing some cardio workout first. Usually, weather permitting, we would take a walk through town before our class.

Even with the sun out the cold was not appealing, so we opted for a more rigorous half-hour of exercise on our treadmill and elliptical machines. Here is what happened:

First, I noticed that I was watching the clock: Uhh-Oh, trying to get it over with... You know... What you resist persists and takes *lonnngger*. I mentioned to Shya that I was clock watching and we began to chat which took our thoughts away from the time. As we moved along, joked and sweated, I came to realize that something had been bothering me since the day before. I had made a couple of mistakes in the last few days. Not big ones, just a red flag that something in me was not quite as crisp as I would have liked. I was not operating from the bull's eye of my own personal center.

I mentioned it to Shya. I told him the little details that were plaguing my thoughts. Here is what he had to say: "Ariel, slow down. Just a little bit. You are trying to do too much, too fast."

And that was that. We finished our workout at home and then went to work out with our trainer. Class was fun. I didn't try to get it over with. I exercised to the best of my ability and we joked with the trainer (and continued to sweat).

On the way home I felt my body rest back against the seat. I took time to look out the windows. I watched the trucks and cars in the lanes next to us. And then, as we took our exit off Route 78, I gazed out my window and saw a majestic creature walking down the edge of the nearby service road. It was a male ring-necked pheasant, a stately bird, roughly the size of a rooster.

"Oh, Shya, a beautiful pheasant! Don't go home – turn right. You have to see it!"

Shya made a right, gliding our car to a stop near the most beautiful pheasant I had ever seen. He sported long tail feathers. His head, neck and chest were iridescent turquoise, green and cobalt blue with a patch of bright scarlet splashed around his eyes. I rolled down my window and we sat and looked at him and he looked at us. Then he took his time strolling away into a nearby field.

Shya and I simultaneously reached out and took one another's hand. Sometimes simple things, little moments are so profound. It was as if this bird had given us a gift by allowing us to fill our hearts with his image and essence. He wasn't hurrying off to get something done. He seemed to be saying, "Don't worry. No need to hurry. Everything you need to do today can be accomplished and you can do so with elegance and grace."

Taking your time and being where you are is certainly a blessing. Not only do you get to witness and enjoy life in all its glory, oddly enough, you get more done.

I was reminded once again of something important that day: Sometimes you need to speed up to fully engage and at other times, you need to slow down.

COMMUNICATION

Communication, the act of giving or exchanging information, at its best is an art form. In the following stories, we provide two humorous examples of misunderstandings that can come between folks, even when you are honestly doing your best to express yourself. If you have a sense of humor about the ways that you communicate, it will be far easier to see how you mis-communicate. If you don't judge yourself for what you're doing, you will be able to identify and melt those things that produce results that you don't want, need or appreciate.

THE TOPLESS BAR

Several years ago we were in Quepos, Costa Rica when Marcella told us about her new business. Marcella works at a charter fishing boat company where we had been clients for years. She is a fiery Latin woman with wavy hair and a boisterous nature. We liked to come into the office from time-to-time and sit in the cool of the air conditioning and hear tales of what the fleet of sport fishing boats had caught and released in the previous days.

On one such day, she said to us, "You must come to visit me one evening at my new business! My boyfriend and I have opened a new topless bar. It is up the hill in Manuel Antonio."

She looked so proud. We were surprised.

"Do your bosses here know that you run a topless bar?"

"Oh yes!" She exclaimed. "Maria and Patricio are two of our best customers."

We looked at each other. How could this be? We knew the owners of the fishing company were Italian and perhaps they were more liberal than we knew. She made a topless bar sound so normal, sort of like going to McDonald's or Applebee's.

Trying not to let our eyes dip to her chest as we tried to imagine the scene, one of us tactfully asked, "Do you work at the bar?"

"Oh yes, I do. Mainly weekends but often on weeknights also. We're getting very busy. You can see our restaurant on the right, just after you pass the Barba Roja restaurant. Look for it and come in. I'll give you a free drink. We have all sorts of typical Costa Rican finger foods. You'll like it. You can bring your groups too."

We had a hard time imagining bringing the participants from one of our 10-day transformational courses to a topless bar but we did our best to be gracious.

We left the fishing office that day, amazed that there was a topless bar in the tiny fishing village and its surroundings. We had been coming for years and although there were many bars, sports bars and eateries, we had never heard of or seen such a thing.

As our taxi took us up the hill to our hotel we scanned the road-side for any sign of Marcella's new topless bar but we didn't see a thing. Several trips up and down that road didn't reveal its where-abouts even though she claimed it was easy to find.

The next week we went into the fishing office for the recent news and sat once again in front of Marcella. The conversation took an unexpected turn.

"I looked for you last week at my restaurant," she said.

"Yes, we looked for the sign but didn't see it."

"I was hoping you would come in for some tapas."

"Tapas? What are tapas?"

Marcella looked confused, "Tapas," she said. "You know tapas bar or finger food bar. Food you eat with your fingers. That's what we serve. Tapas is the Costa Rican word for finger food. Obviously that's why we call it a tapas bar."

We burst out laughing and explained the joke. She had been saying tapas, which we understood to be topless since we hadn't heard this word before. Our mental computers just filled in with what they knew as a reasonable facsimile. When we asked her about her "topless" bar, that word was so outside of her reality, she filled in with what she expected to hear, "tapas."

As we left that day, we thought it was a good joke and an excellent example of how we only know what we know and how anything that is outside of our reality doesn't even exist. It also showed us how three people who were sincerely trying to communicate with each other could so totally and utterly misinterpret what was said.

A LITTLE SOMETHING EXTRA

Have you ever wondered how an apparently neutral comment can have a surprisingly unreceptive response? Have you seen how similar situations may arise in different circumstances and what you meant to say produces a reaction that is not what you expected?

What if you are well-intentioned? What if you are actually communicating clearly but, unbeknownst to you, you are adding a little something extra?

Life is certainly funny in that it gives you answers if you pay attention. We were surprised to discover the answers to some of our client's questions about their relationships when we leased a new car. Here is Shya's account of what happened:

When we leased our Suburban it had many amenities, air conditioning, heated seats, automatic windows and power locks. It was late June when we took possession of the vehicle and the winter warming package was not yet necessary, but I looked forward to being able to settle into a nice warm seat on bitter-cold mornings.

With the mere touch of a button the windows glided down. With another button, the seats had memory so I could preset them. With a tap of another button the mirrors would adjust to how each of us liked them. The gas and brake pedals were also adjustable so that

118

Ariel, whose legs are shorter than mine, didn't have to hug the dashboard in order to reach them.

The summer days were warm during the "break-in" period as we were getting to know the car. Suddenly, inexplicably, my legs would get warm and my back would stick to the seat in a sweaty slick. It was as if the sun had snuck behind me in a sudden burst of radiant heat. Even though cool air was blowing over me, I had a hot backside so I quickly looked for the source. The discomfort could be traced back to me. The little something extra I had done, while rolling down the window, had immediate and palpable consequences.

It turns out that the driver's seat heating button was located on the door, next to the window button and power locks, squeezed-in, near the buttons that adjusted the mirror. To my chagrin, I discovered that it was oh-so-easy to inadvertently bump the seatheating switch with a flick of a little finger as I was rolling down the window. Then before I knew what had happened I would be sweltering in my seat. Since the heating unit itself is so efficient, it takes some time to cool off.

I had to chuckle each time I sat in the "hot seat." It was a little embarrassing to know I had caused my own discomfort but as I looked at the situation from an anthropological prespective I learned something. In other words, I didn't judge myself for turning the seat on, I just became interested in the phenomenon.

Here is what I discovered: I realized that I wasn't "communicating" incorrectly. The door buttons didn't misinterpret my intent. Each time I made my move I successfully made the window raise or lower. It was easy to see that I simply added something extra to the move. With the awareness that I could initiate a response from the car that I didn't want, I could adjust my actions so that things didn't get warm.

Take a look at lighted exit signs. They glow red in the dark to light up the way out of movie theaters and other buildings. But, in truth, the light is white and the filter the light goes through gives it a red appearance. Folks often don't realize that their communications come through a filter of their experience and prejudices and seemingly simple comments can cause another's blood to boil.

I rarely bump the seat warmer button these days when I roll down the window. I've learned the ways of my car. But when I inadvertently add that little something extra, I still smile when I realize that getting mad at my car or being angry with myself won't change the fact that in that moment, I have unintentionally created a situation that I don't like.

When people can see that adding something extra to their communication causes much of the trouble in their ability to relate, if they don't judge themselves for what they see, then they don't have to keep putting themselves in the hot seat.

BEING HERE

Our friend, Harry, accompanied a friend of his into a bank foyer one Sunday as she needed to use her ATM card to get some cash. As he stood there waiting for her to finish her transaction, he was lost in a muddle of thoughts about his day – what to do, how to behave, how to do things "right." Suddenly he realized that he wasn't standing where he was. He had lost all sense of his surroundings.

Dropping the internal conversation he looked around and saw the walls and the textures, the sun pouring through the windows and the wind whipping the trees outside. Then he noticed an old man standing in that small foyer with him. The man had been there all along but Harry had been so consumed by his thoughts it was as if this gentleman had appeared from nowhere. Harry gave him a smile and realized that the elderly man looked disoriented or confused.

"Do you need help sir?" Harry asked.

"Yes, the bank. This is a bank. Is it open?"

Realizing the source of the man's confusion Harry replied, "Yes, it is a bank. But this is Sunday. The bank is closed today."

"Ah, it's closed. It's Sunday. I forgot." Relief flooded the old man's face as he turned and moved out into the day.

Harry told us it was one of the most profound moments of his life, a moment of enlightenment. In an instant he recognized that the incident with this man was something he would never forget. At first, he found this confusing as it was so simple. Nothing big. Not like the birth of his child or other highly significant events of his life. And then Harry realized the difference. It wasn't because he had been helping someone. He regularly helps customers in his bistro and he is kind to friends and strangers alike. This is part of his nature. Harry realized that what made that moment so precious was simply that he was there, *really there*.

You don't have to get anywhere in order to have your life be profoundly satisfying. It simply takes *Being Here*. This next section demonstrates that in everyday situations, even while doing mundane things, there are magical lessons waiting to be discovered in each moment.

MARY AND INSPIRATION

One autum in the late eighties found us at the New York Pathwork Center, a retreat center cradled in the Catskill Mountains. There were little sleeping bungalows for participants, a course room, and the dining hall where they served vegetarian food; kind-of a holistic sleep-away camp for big kids. Our course room, a former barn, boasted big vaulted ceilings, sliding glass doors and lots of light. We sat on the floor on big cushions that were strewn around the perimeter of the room.

The weekend we met Mary, we were presenting "The Freedom to Breathe" and "The Art of Being a Healer," two courses we often offer in concert since they are so compatible.

The first day was devoted to allowing yourself to fall into the moment by using a breathing technique. This is a spiritual adventure with a partner. Half of the day you are engaging in the technique and the other half you are simply being there as a support for your friend. It's amazing how nurturing it can be to get the attention of another human being for no other reason than the fact that you are breathing. Folks generally rediscover that it isn't what they do that makes the difference but rather who they are and that simply being there is what matters. From both positions you get to experience giving and receiving, and sample a taste of the mystical nature of life itself.

The second day was "The Art of Being a Healer." This course is nourishing, especially after spending a whole day massaging yourself from the inside with your breath. Early on we realized that if a person could get into the moment, direct their attention to what was happening in his or her body, be willing to be with the sensations or emotions found there and let go of the story about why the feelings were there in the first place, a profound healing could take place. We also developed this course recognizing that people want to make a difference and that regardless of what you do in life, if you are present, you become a healing presence in your own life and in the lives of others. We regularly have people from all walks of life participate in these two courses. People go home from this weekend enlivened and inspired. We have heard it said that it is more refreshing than a week's vacation. But little did we know, the inspiration that one participant, Mary, would find on this particular weekend. We could not have guessed the healing that she and her daughter, Christine, who joined her there, were looking for.

We all arrived on a Friday afternoon in October and the day was sunny and surprisingly crisp. The sun had already moved lower on the horizon as fall advanced and this meant that direct sunlight shown on the valley only from 9:30 a.m. to 4:00 p.m. or so. A wave of giant maples streaked the hillside crimson. The trees near the barn were laden with red apples and deer leisurely wandered through, nibbling the windfalls and plucking the ripe ones from the lower branches. There was small stream on the property which was a perfect place for a quiet stroll or a peaceful contemplation with nature. The water flashed, rich with gold medallions as it swirled with leaves floating downstream.

Everyone arrived in the nearby town of Phoenicia by bus or by car in the early afternoon with enough time to get to the facility, check in and make their way to the barn before the sun dipped behind the rolling hills. Most of the participants we knew from previous weekends or evening groups in New York City, but there were a few folks we were meeting for the first time – Mary and her daughter Christine were among them.

Dressed comfortably in denim jeans and a flannel shirt over a t-shirt, Mary was a slim woman in her late forties, with wispy graying auburn hair pulled into a ponytail. Christine had a slightly round face, straight light brown shoulder length hair and what looked like a small diamond stud in her right nostril. While nose piercing was not unheard of in the late 80s, it was rare and it looked slightly incongruous with Christine's sprinkling of freckles and clear, green eyes.

That afternoon, we sat in a loose circle and introductions began. People let each other know what drew them to the seminar, where they lived and what they hoped for themselves from participating that weekend. It was a rich and vital time where each person figuratively threw his or her hat in the ring and said, "I'm here. This is me. Count me in."

Of course, it is up to each individual how much to reveal. It only made sense that folks who had known us longer were, in general, more comfortable with the process and tended to be a bit more verbally expressive in their introductions.

When we sat down, Mary and Christine sat directly across from us and while they had yet to say much to us personally or out loud to the group, their body language spoke volumes; two opposite magnets, repelling each other yet straining towards one another at the same time. The air seemed to shimmer between them with tension and history and need. As we went around the circle and one after another the folks made themselves known, you could see both mother and daughter relaxing into themselves and into each other, two undernourished beings turning to the light.

"I am Amy," the bright young woman next to Mary said. "I would come to any weekend offered by the Kanes but my husband and I love this weekend in particular. It is such a break from Wall Street and teaching people how to program computers. I could use the rest!" People chuckled, heads nodding in agreement. "I've been looking forward to this weekend for weeks and I'm really happy to be here."

She turned to Mary with a smiling invitation. Taking a breath, Mary looked around and said in a quiet voice. "I am here to spend some time with my daughter Christine and to be here and breathe and be myself. I hope that's enough."

"Being yourself is enough for us," we replied. "Hopefully you will discover that it's more than enough for you."

"How did you find out about this weekend?" Amy asked.

"A friend told me that if I wanted to have a deep, intimate experience of myself, a workshop with the Kanes was just the place to go. I called them on the phone last week and they told me about this weekend and it fit my time frame and my needs perfectly. I immediately felt a connection with Ariel and Shya and I am really happy I was able to make it.

"This is my daughter, Christine. I drove up from the Philadelphia area and she flew in from Ohio to join me. I could really use this weekend to breathe," she said with a slightly mysterious smile and it seemed that Mary was looking inward, enjoying a private joke.

When Christine went next, she echoed her mother — she was here mainly to spend some quality time with Mary.

As the little valley became more and more shaded, we met each and every participant. We all settled in and slowed down from our hectic lives and took time to breathe.

"Tomorrow morning," we told everyone, "we'll meet here after breakfast at 9:30 a.m. Be sure to wear comfortable and layered clothing so that if you get too cool or too warm, you can adjust. If anyone needs anything in their room, don't hesitate to see us before you go, either now or at dinner. Dinner is at 7:00 p.m. which gives you time to hang out with each other and enjoy this glorious afternoon. Anyone who has any medical conditions or health concerns, even if we know about them, be sure to take a moment before you leave the course room and tell us or remind us about it so we know if you need some special attention. Other than that, we'll see you all at dinner."

Some people lay back on the cushions and made themselves comfortable and others helped each other get up and headed outside. I saw Amy ask her husband, Andy, to reach up and pluck an apple from a high branch of a tree. She rubbed it on her pant leg before they moved down the hill toward the stream.

In ones and twos the remaining folks came to see us. Some for hugs and greetings, others to let us know of asthma or allergies or other medical concerns. In the end, only Mary and Christine were still reclining on their cushions, quietly chatting with one another. We looked at them and Mary seemed smaller now and pale. Looking at one another, with a nod, we went and sat with them.

"Nice to meet you both in person," we said and handshakes were exchanged, pleasantries offered.

"Mary, are you all right? You look a little pale."

Christine leaned closer to her mom, tilted her head and waited.

"Ariel and Shya, I am glad we have a moment alone," Mary said with a warm smile, directed to her daughter. "I must admit I do have a medical condition."

We calmly waited. Christine reached out and took her mother's hand.

127

"See, I have cancer," she said and her smile faltered just a bit. "It's terminal. I have a large tumor right here," she said, pointing to her breastbone, just below her heart, "and it is resting on my aorta. There is nothing the doctors can do at this point. In fact, they don't want me to be here. They don't want me to be anywhere but in the hospital, waiting for my death. But I want to live, really live. I know I am pale. The tumor is so large that I can't get enough oxygen anymore. So you see, I really do need the freedom to breathe. If you don't mind, I would like to have this time with my daughter. We haven't been too close over the years." Christine squeezed her hand, and the nose diamond flashed. "I don't know how you pair people up, but we would like to be partners tomorrow."

"You two can certainly be partners. That is not a problem. But, tell us more about your condition. We are not experts in medicine and obviously we are not physicians. We want to make sure we are being responsible, not only for you, but also for the well-being of everyone this weekend."

Mary grinned. It was a thousand watt smile. Our hearts melted, not that they needed any extra help at this point. "Don't worry about me. I'll be fine. I've got at least two weeks left, so they tell me. There aren't any expected complications. At some point soon, the tumor will get too big and then I will need to be put on oxygen and then, well, I won't need anything. I just want to give myself all the living I can until I go. And I want to spend some quality time with my daughter, too. Time is what I have to give her, and not much at that."

Now it was Christine's turn to look pale. She knew the truth of the situation but hearing her mother say it so directly brought reality into focus.

"Don't worry," she said, "I know what to do if Mom starts failing. I have her medicine, all of the numbers of her doctors, and I already got information on local medical assistance. We won't need it, though. Mom is stubborn that way." With this she lifted her chin — a challenge, with dignity, her eyes softly glistening.

No need for us to talk it over. We were intimately familiar with cancer and its devastation. As a child, Shya's sister had died of spinal cancer. Then, years later after the two of us had married and ultimately moved to Woodstock, we had become reacquainted with an old friend of Shya's in the local supermarket who died of cancer a short time later.

"Bernie Kagan," Shya had shouted down the line at the grocery check out counter when he spotted his old friend. "You stole my bow!"

Bernie whirled around in surprise, "Shya Kane! I still have it in my garage. Come and get it!"

Bernie was a fellow from Shya's childhood who 30 years prior had borrowed a bow and some arrows from him. Shortly thereafter, he and his parents had moved so he had never returned them. The two adolescents, now men, had not seen each other since that time but the memory and connection had remained.

We didn't want the bow back, although Bernie did, indeed, still have it. But it turned out to be a device to renew a friendship after all those years. Bernie was now a local real estate agent in our area and there were signs along the road advertising houses for sale. Little placards sat on several of them, advertising the company showing the house and the agent in charge. Bernie's placard said, "If you need help, call Bernie Kagan." It became a running gag between the two of us when we passed one of the signs to call out, "Berr-nee Kaay-gan!"

A few months after our reunion, Bernie discovered that he had cancer and the prognosis was not good. We went to visit him at his home.

"Bernie, why don't you come down to one of our transformational seminars while you still have the energy," Shya said. "Use it to find some closure for yourself. Give yourself the opportunity to experience a sense of peace. Consider it a going away present."

Bernie was grateful for the offer. He really was. And he was terrified. He didn't accept our gift and we had no hard feelings. Of course, his was a highly personal journey and he needed to make his own choices as best he could. As the months progressed, so did his disease and we would visit him periodically watching his health decline. Shya would gently massage his feet and Bernie would talk about his failing kidneys and his body shutting down. All the while, his terror of death and the unknown steadily grew, unabated, just like his cancer. He set up hospice at his home and a close friend moved in to help. It turned out, however, that she was angry at the disease, angry he was dying, angry at her helplessness and she aimed it at everyone who visited, accusing them of not doing enough to help him get well. The last time we saw Bernie, she was making a green protein concoction and railing against Bernie's circumstances. When we left that day, the next wave of supporters came to the door and the tirade began again.

At night, we would lie in bed cuddling and there we would quietly discuss how much we wished Bernie had taken advantage of our going away gift. It was hard to watch him back then, in so much pain and uncertainty and fear.

Now, as Mary sat before us, dreaming of fully living what was left of her life and sharing the magic of those moments with her daughter, we didn't think twice.

"Of course, you two can be partners. Just take care of yourself this weekend, Mary. During the "Freedom To Breathe," we will encourage people to breathe deeply and with intensity. Make sure to move at your own pace. Don't try to keep up with anyone else.

Just do what is right for you and your condition. If either of you need anything let us know right away. We are staying in the cottage just on the other side of the dining hall. It is the little white building with the name, "trillium," over the door. We are available to you, day or night. We will leave it up to you whether or not you tell the other participants about the tumor, OK?"

Mary and Christine smiled simultaneously. We all stood up and headed out into the afternoon. The air seemed clearer. Yellow jackets feasted on fallen apples. Crickets sang lustily. A chill was in the air. Winter was coming.

Dinner was lively. Ours was not the only course on the roster that weekend. There was a men's group and other events. Brigita was in charge of the kitchen and she ruled there with an iron fist and the occasional threat. Because the kitchen itself wasn't locked in the evenings, she had taken to leaving signs to stop unwanted pilfering of sweets and supplies. A crude scull and cross bones were drawn on paper signs hanging over plates full of peanut butter and chocolate chip cookies. It read, "On pain of DEATH do not take more than one cookie each!"

The two of us took our allotment and went to our room while participants hung out over cups of tea.

The next morning was chilly and clear, the grass laden with dew, the robins migrating south. We all met in the barn and so began "The Freedom to Breathe." The participants partnered up and as the morning session got underway, Mary lay down for the technique while Christine sat next to her.

We encouraged people to breathe with intensity. As we did, our usual words took on far greater meaning. "Breathe in with a little more volume and a little faster than your usual rhythm. Go for it as if your life depended on it."

"When you breathe out, don't keep anything back. Don't keep a reserve. Really let it all go."

"Each breath is a perfect life cycle. When you took your first breath that is how they knew you were alive. Letting go of your last breath is the last thing you will do. So give yourself everything with each breath. Breathe in life to its fullest and when you cannot take in anymore, let it go."

By now tears were running freely down Christine's cheeks. We handed her tissues and took some for ourselves.

"Inspire yourself. Inspiration as in: To breathe life into."

The day progressed. People laughed and cried. Most felt deeply and some felt very little as they drifted on each breath.

After lunch, it was the afternoon session and Christine's turn. She lay on the carpeted floor, with an old quilt for extra padding. She looked young and vulnerable lying there. Of course she wasn't alone since there were many pairs of breathing partners scattered around the barn. And of course there was her mother, Mary, who looked very Madonna-like as she sat, legs tucked beneath her, hands folded in her lap. Perhaps sweetest of all, Mary's cheeks were rosy. She was flushed with life.

The afternoon sun slanted through the high windows, dust motes dancing, sunbeams spotlighting someone's hair here and warming toes there. We played music and started the breathing process once again.

When it was over, folks sat up looking renewed. Each and every individual came away looking scrubbed clean, from the inside out. It was a powerful and moving day.

The evening meal was more subdued and more vibrant, all at the same time. Food had more taste, the colors and aromas richer.

Eventually, raccoons begged for cookies by the back door.

The next morning, "The Art of Being a Healer" day started. Folks arrived early, some with coffee in hand, steaming in the chill air. A sense of camaraderie had developed. New friendships had been made, old ones strengthened.

We began by asking to hear something from everyone. People, visibly lighter and more rested, talked of the air and the leaves and sleeping well. Morning walks had invigorated them, they had enjoyed a healthy breakfast and we were ready for another day of transformation.

"We are not going to start right away with bodywork. No sense working with each other unless you are *here* while being with your partners. Let's talk about the art of being a healer."

We discussed healing in general, why people had pain and the New Agey belief that if you are ill, you caused it by doing your life wrong. We talked about how the story of "why you are the way you are" will keep you stuck in your condition. And through it all we watched Mary. We didn't stare at her, of course, but it was hard not to notice how much she kept teetering on the edge of making her illness known to the others. Finally, with a big breath, she leapt. And when she did, she was mesmerizing.

"I know about pain and I know about illness. I have been ill for some time now. I have tried all sorts of modalities, both traditional and New Age, to heal myself and I have come to realize that healing and being a healer does not necessarily mean that your body is healthy."

Mary was still dancing around the issue but you could tell she wanted to be more direct. She got a gentle nudge from Amy.

"What do you mean that you are ill?" Amy asked straight out but with an innocence that made the question unobtrusive.

133

"I have cancer. And my body is really sick. In fact I am dying. I don't like to talk about it much because I don't want anyone's pity. And I don't want the judgments either. I don't know why I got sick. But I do know that life is precious. I do know that every minute counts. I am very clear that some situations cannot be changed but how I meet this situation makes all the difference." And now she grinned, "It is really, really good to be alive."

And so the course continued. People were respectful of Mary and of her disease and she of them. Everyone, regardless of his or her health, left that weekend enlivened.

That was the last we saw of Mary. A few months later, we received a small pink card postmarked from San Diego, California. It was a hand written note from Christine.

Dear Ariel and Shya,

I thought you would want to know that my mother's passing was gentle. She died about a month after we met you both. She died at home.

We were both profoundly grateful that we came to your weekend. We had never been close, often fought. But after the weekend, I got to be with her until the end.

You are right. Transformation is instantaneous. It was as if all of those bad years never existed. It was a sweet time for us both. I have moved to California now and am going back to school. My mother and I both thank you.
Christine

We found ourselves smiling as a sense of peace descended upon us when we read Christine's note. Perhaps this peace was a little parting gift to us from Mary. We were so happy for both Mary and

Christine. Many people live on this earth but so few take the opportunity to *really* live. Mary, even on death's doorstep, realized that each breath and each day was too precious to waste. That she found the freedom to breathe and the freedom to be herself was a miracle. It was a true blessing that she shared these moments in her final days with Christine and was kind enough to include all of us as well.

There are many people who go through life with regrets about things they didn't say to a person whom they have loved and lost. Many have incompletions with one parent or the other. It is impossible to live to one's full potential and experience the fullness that life has to offer when walking around with resentments and regrets. It was so sweet that Mary and Christine had a chance to realize the perfection of their relationship together.

We have not crossed paths with Christine in the ensuing years. We don't know what she went back to study or where she went from there. But we do know that her time with Mary set her up to win in her life and the weekend spent together in such an intimate way was a graceful springboard into her future.

FINDING THE BALANCE POINT

Most people aim to live in a way that produces a sense of well-being, satisfaction and accomplishment. We are all interested in being productive and achieving the goals that are consistent with our values. However, the two of us have often observed that in the desire to attain their goals, people often lose sight of what is happening in their lives... in each moment. People are driven to accomplish what they think will produce happiness, success and well-being and miss all that life has to offer when you are *Being Here.*

We are not suggesting that you should not have goals. It is simply that focusing on future goals will rob you of the richness of this moment.

Here is an example:

Since we are both avid fly fishers, we took a short vacation after one of our winter seminars in Costa Rica, where we set out to catch large Pacific sailfish on fly rods. There we hired Captain Bobby, his boat and mate to take us off the Costa Rican coast in the blue Pacific in search of these majestic creatures.

Each year, for the previous four years, we had fished with Captain Bobby. When we first met him, he was working for a fishing lodge as one of their premier guides. We seemed to get along well together, so we continued to book trips with him after he went into business for himself.

It was just Bobby, his mate and the two of us, on a 26-foot boat, heading off shore for an adventure near Golfito, Costa Rica. There is something about the intensity and immediacy of life at sea that fascinates and feeds us.

Each day began at dawn as we motored away from the small village nestled next to the rain forest and out between the arms of land that guard Golfito. As we headed out to sea, we always encountered something vital. There were majestic trees on shore that burst into purple blossoms and the fragrance wafted out on the breeze. We often came upon giant schools of dolphins that jumped and cavorted, swimming in front of the bow of the boat, a marine vanguard of some of the most intelligent creatures on the planet. There were big gray ones, sleek and powerful, effortlessly gliding, gracing our craft with their presence, elegantly taking turns leading us to wherever our bow was pointed. There were also the spinner dolphins that treated us to aerial acrobatic displays as they jumped and spun, twirling in apparent delight before splashing back into the sea. The spinners are often accompanied by yellowfin tuna and they work together corralling and feeding upon the schools of small baitfish. You can see this group from a long distance. It is a frenzy of glistening water, leaping shapes and a raucous cloud of diving seabirds.

Sea turtles are more sedate. They poke their heads above water to watch the world go by. Occasionally, we have had a spectacular view of whales, up close and personal. On one particular trip, we saw a mother and her calf speeding toward the distant shore. They leapt and dove in tandem on a path parallel to our boat. For some time we kept pace with these giants.

Manta rays do back flips, frigate birds soar high on the thermals and pelicans fly in formation inches above the waves as they catch the updrafts. And then, there are the big game fish, dorado, Pacific sailfish and marlin. The dorado are golden, blue green bullets that streak from the deep to attack the lures that are trolled behind the boat. Sailfish materialize, thrashing about as they attempt to stun the bait with their beaks, so that they can have a leisurely feed. And the marlins are the kings – creatures without equal. These amazingly powerful and aggressive goliaths emerge from nowhere at full fury; suddenly the deceptively passive skin of the water erupts as something the size of a small car explodes into view.

Sometimes on one of these trips, we have come upon a log, floating like a solitary world 20 or 30 miles from anything, a whole ecosystem unto itself. Birds sit and rest. Crabs and shrimp-like creatures scuttle on its surface and below, in the shadow of the log itself, descending layers of baitfish circle and feed upon the smaller life forms. The dorado, sailfish and marlin can lurk just out of view waiting to pounce.

So our "fishing" expeditions are immersions into the life and grandeur of the sea. Each day on the water is a gift, full of sights, sounds and smells that allow us to get back in touch with nature and the vastness of life on the planet.

You would think that being a fishing captain would be a very fulfilling way to lead life. But Captain Bobby was blinded by a revolving set of goals. When we first met him, he would complain about the management of the lodge and say, "If I had my own boat, I would do it differently. I would do things better than they do."

On this particular trip, Bobby had finally accomplished some of his life long ambitions, including getting a boat of his own. His current goal, which he enticed us to be a part of, was to capture a world record sized fish on a fly rod. Bobby was very interested in Ariel becoming the new women's world record holder for Pacific sailfish and so our days included attaining this goal. It became an exciting adventure to hunt for big game, hoping to catch one that was the biggest ever recorded. One day, Ariel caught that big fish. It was truly a giant. A grizzled beast weighing well over 100 pounds, almost 10 feet long from tip to tail.

We had won. We had accomplished what we had set out to do. The euphoria lasted almost an entire evening. Then the trouble began. Bobby had met one of his own personal goals and so it was on to the next one with a fervor and intensity of purpose. What we discovered was that he was no longer just fishing and enjoying the wealth of experience to be had on the ocean. We were now fiercely directed into "must get another world's record" as if the attainment of this goal would produce some sense of real and lasting satisfaction.

A few days later, Ariel caught a world record size roosterfish. That night at dinner Bobby let us know that this was one of his four life goals. Things after that went from somewhat bad to worse. He became irritable, easily frustrated and quick to anger. Now we couldn't do it right enough for him, nor could we catch a big enough fish, fast enough. Fishing became serious business. No more "Mr. Nice Guy." We talked to him about this, of course, since it was not our idea of fun on vacation. He wasn't so open about his frustration during the rest of the trip but we could see it seething just below the surface.

Bobby had gotten lost in the idea that attaining the next goal would somehow fulfill him, validate his existence and make him a happier person. The problem with this idea arises when you actually attain your objective. Life is not fundamentally changed by achievement. And so the accomplishment of a goal, under these circumstances, does not produce a sense of well-being or satisfaction.

If you are satisfied in yourself, the attainment of a goal is satisfying. If you are not satisfied, the attainment of a goal only stimulates the need for the next one. The completion of something intensifies who you are and how you are currently being. So, if the attainment of a goal is about expressing yourself into life, then your feeling of self-expression, self-worth and well-being is intensified. If, however, you are producing goals because you feel you are deficient or inadequate, coming from the fantasy that the attainment of your desires will produce satisfaction or sufficiency, when you reach your objective, you will be disappointed. The sense of emptiness or dissatisfaction becomes stronger.

Having goals can be extremely useful but not if they are attained while sacrificing your experience of living in each moment. If you are worrying about the future and the production of goals, you cannot be engaged in what is happening in this current moment in your life.

Our fishing story is a prime example. Catching big game fish requires more than just the angler's skill. It is a team effort and having a mutual goal kept all of us focused and gave meaning and purpose to our actions. Mistakes were minimized because we brought all of our attention and ability to the process of catching fish. But there is a balance point. Focus is a benefit, but if you are off in the future, expecting the outcome to produce long-term happiness or satisfaction, you miss the magic of the moment and life becomes serious and two-dimensional.

Ariel ultimately caught three world record fish during that trip, two Pacific sailfish and one roosterfish. She currently holds numerous Women's Fly Fishing World Records with The International Game Fish Association.

BUT I WANT TO BE AN ARTIST!
As told by Ariel

One fall, we held one of our business courses called "Transformation in the Workplace," in New York City. Folks from all different fields were there to discover how to be more effective, productive and satisfied in their jobs.

On this particular weekend we had a full range of occupations represented – homemaker, lawyer, entrepreneur, banker, doctor, secretary, teacher, actor, professor, etc. As the weekend progressed, we explored what it takes to experience well-being on the job, and how to effectively communicate. We also heard each person's reasons for attending and what they hoped to achieve.

As we went around the room, we met Nancy, a business owner who was there with her entire staff, hoping to build an even stronger team. Charlotte, a dental hygienist and nutritional consultant, wanted to be able to balance both jobs and make more money from her nutrition business. As we spoke with Charlotte, a soft looking man in his mid-forties, Jonathan, sat up straighter in his chair. He was totally engaged in the conversation and since we had read his questionnaire, we knew what he was grappling with. Jonathan had a double life – at least in his own mind. A computer software engineer at a Fortune 500 company during the day, he was a professional musician by night. For Jonathan, these two occupations did not peacefully co-exist.

When our conversation with Charlotte concluded, Shya asked who wanted to speak next. Without missing a beat, Jonathan leapt to his feet shouting out, "I do." He grinned and folks chuckled at his exuberance.

"My name is Jonathan and I work at a large bank, running a bunch of their computer systems. I make a lot of money there, but I'm not happy. See, I'm also a professional musician. I play the clarinet, I compose and I'm part of a jazz ensemble. I play in symphonies and for shows, and I find that working during the day exhausts me and ruins my playing."

"How so?" Shya asked.

"Well, Shya, at the end of the day I'm too tired to practice. I play my clarinet, but most of the time it's lackluster and I make mistakes. I know if I wasn't so worn out from working at my ?*$%^&# job I could play better. I go to gigs now and I'm uninspired. I'm thinking of quitting the bank, but I have a family to think of and the money is so good. I also have a 401K plan but I don't want to sell out for money. I want to be the artist that I know I am!"

As he spoke, Jonathan had worked himself up, his face flushed with passion. Others in the room were nodding as the professional actors and directors could empathize with how day-to-day work gets in the way of being artistic. You could see it written on their faces, *If only I could just act rather than have to get jobs, then I would be happy.*

"How is the quality of your playing these days Jonathan?" Shya asked.

"Stale, Shya," he said sadly. "Stale."

"Well, Albert Einstein once said that you can't solve a problem from within the system that created it," Shya continued. "It sounds as if your possible solutions to your dilemma, stay and be stale or leave your job and forfeit benefits, will both result in creating problems. With transformation there is no downside."

It was clear that Jonathan liked the sound of anything that would solve his problem without the downside.

"I have a suggestion for an experiment," I said. "But it will involve taking a risk. Are you ready?"

"Oh, yes!" he replied. It was obvious from his face that he hoped we would finally give him the permission he had not granted himself to chuck the job and his responsibilities to his family. Then, he could go for being a full-time musician at last. His eyes glowed with anticipation.

Shya and I glanced at each other and I continued, "Here is what we suggest. For the next two weeks, forget about your clarinet. Put it away."

"Let go of all thoughts of being a musician," Shya said.

Jonathan's face fell and he looked ready to fight. He was sure we were just like his parents who didn't want him to go for his truth. He thought we wanted him to do the sensible thing, the boring thing, the nine-to-five thing. He opened his mouth to protest as I finished the thought.

"...and at the end of these two weeks, see how this has improved your ability to play and how much it enhances your abilities as a musician."

Jonathan repeatedly opened and closed his mouth in disbelief.

"Wait a minute. Ariel, Shya, are you suggesting not playing for two weeks as a way to improve my musicianship?"

"Yup, exactly," I said.

"But, how is that going to help? I mean, I need to be disciplined and practice in order to improve."

Shya took over from there, "Well see, Jonathan, you said things were stale, right?"

"Yes."

"And I can assume that you have been disciplined for years and that you have followed the prescription of diligently practicing. But you aren't happy or satisfied or productive either at work or with your clarinet?"

"True, Shya, so true."

"Well, what do you have to lose? Are you willing to give it a go?"

Jonathan nodded slowly. He looked confused and he wasn't sure what good it would do, but he was willing.

"That's great, Jonathan," I said. "When you get home, put your clarinet in its case, and put away your music, your music stand and everything you associate with playing and practicing. For the next two weeks, pretend that your clarinet and your skills as a musician do not exist. You may think about it at first, but if you find your mind wandering there, bring your attention back to what you're doing. OK?"

"Absolutely, I'll do it!" he pronounced with the same kind of enthusiasm he had demonstrated in the first place.

The course continued and came to its natural conclusion. We saw Jonathan at a couple of our weekly Monday evening seminars during the next two weeks, but no one mentioned his experiment. We all were operating as if his clarinet did not exist and no one wanted to remind him of the process. Two weeks quickly came and went and on the following Monday Jonathan joined us once again for the seminar, but this time there was a bounce in his step and a glimmer in his eye.

At the first opportunity, Jonathan stood and spoke. I noticed he was standing taller and looked more grounded in himself.

"I am so excited," he announced. "Two weeks ago, Ariel and Shya gave me the weirdest, neatest, strangest, most inspired suggestion I have ever had in my life. OK, so here's the background: I work at a bank and I'm also a musician. I've been playing the clarinet since I was a child, but for the past few years, particularly the last six months, there was no joy in it for me. I came to the Kanes' business course hoping to find a way to bring some life back into my playing as I feel like I've been doing everything by rote lately.

I was shocked when they suggested that I put the clarinet and all my music away for two weeks and pretend it didn't exist. I mean, I'm a pro! What kind of professional lets it slide for two weeks and expects to be able to play well?"

At this he grinned, folks smiled and I could see he was letting things build to a crescendo. Now he turned his sparkling eyes our way, "Ariel, Shya, I took my music and stand and clarinet out of the closet yesterday. It had been two weeks and a day! They were all so familiar and yet so new. I was excited to be able to pick a song and test the reed and I realized that I hadn't felt this kind of spark for a long, long time. I ran through my warm up exercises and my fingers flew. Music flowed out of the tips of my fingers and the tone was so pure, I played for an hour without stopping and it seemed like just a moment had passed. All I can say is: Wow! And, thank you both."

"How was work the past two weeks?" Shya asked.

"It's a little embarrassing how well I did. I guess I've always held a piece of myself back at the bank. I know it sounds irrational but it seemed that if I succeeded there I might get stuck in a nine-to-five job and I might lose my creative juice. I've always been holding back with the hope of being an artist."

"Are you an artist and did your work these past two weeks take away from that?" I asked.

"Yes, yes I am an artist and no, working at the bank didn't take anything away. In fact, I did things far faster than I ever thought possible this past week. I created new solutions to some old programming problems that we've been having for a while now. Even my boss noticed the difference. He stopped at my workstation yesterday and thanked me for a new piece of software I wrote. That has never happened before."

"See Jonathan," Shya said. "If you hold back your full expression of yourself in one area, you gradually get dimmer in all areas of your life, including or maybe especially in those areas you're trying to protect. Life is like a magnificent river and it takes energy to stop the flow. Going about your life with excellence in your 'day' job turns it into a brilliant experience and it then becomes a creative act. As you go about your life with totality you become an artist wherever you go and whatever you do."

We looked around the room as Jonathan sat down and saw people quietly nodding to themselves. There were others there who had been using one reason or another to hold back and it was easy to see the sparkle being rekindled in their eyes, too, just thinking of going about their days with totality. Transformation had happened with Jonathan and it had just happened, again, as he shared with everyone about his successful experiment in being where he was, rather than holding out for that special time and the better activity. We knew he had just made a difference in many people's lives but the results would show up in the days ahead. Transformation is like that. The shift happens and then, if you are present and watch for it, you get to see the results.

As the evening came to an end, we could feel a surge of enthusiasm in the buzz of conversation as people left for the night. By the next Monday, people came back with more things to ask and share and Jonathan came back and he still looked aglow. Soon a young actor, Raul, who happened to be seated just next to Jonathan, stood with a big smile.

"I owe you all, and Jonathan in particular, a big thank you!" he said. "I borrowed your experiment, Jonathan, I hope you don't mind." Jonathan grinned as Raul continued, "I am an actor and I have always hated my day job as a waiter. I wait tables in mid-town, mostly for the lunch rush and I've always thought it was a colossal waste of time, especially as I've always thought I should be out auditioning and advancing my career during the day. Not that I've really been productive at doing that on my days off, but I always had the fantasy. So, I was a resentful guy and made my customers pay. If they wanted even something as simple as a napkin, I would bring them one with attitude. I know, I know, that isn't such a great way to get tips, but I always thought I was too good for that job and I wanted people to know my frustration." Raul paused and looked around at his audience. We were swept away by his "performance" and ready for the next scene.

"So here is what I did this week. When I was waiting tables, I forgot about being an actor. I made as if this was all I was, and all I had, and I went about it with excellence. On Thursday, I waited on a table where two women were seated and I took really good care of them. I honestly wanted them to have a great dining experience. I wanted them to leave enlivened. At the end of the meal, one of the ladies said, 'Wow, you really took care of us. You are great. What a nice meal. Are you an actor?' When I told her that I was she said, 'I am a casting director. Here is my card. Please send me your resume this week. Lots of people look the part when I am casting, but with your attitude, you're just the type of actor I'm looking to hire.'

I dropped my resume at her office the very next day and I have my first audition next week. I don't know if anything will come from it but I do know that I feel better about myself than ever. I have discovered I love being of service and I even really like waiting tables!"

People at the Monday night group broke into spontaneous applause. Raul was radiant. After a moment, he pulled Jonathan to his feet and to the delight of all present, like true artists, they both took a bow.

DETROIT SHARON
As told by Shya

As I look back some 40 odd years, I am amazed at how fresh these events appear in my memory. I was 21 years old, scheduled to take a semester of courses at the University of Hawaii and I was leaving in about three weeks. At that time I was completing some classes at New York University and my next-door neighbor, Wendy, had a girlfriend who was visiting from their hometown of Detroit. Her name was Sharon. She was very, very cute – short dark hair, large eyes, and a petite, sexy body. We were immediately attracted to each other.

We quickly discovered that I was leaving in three weeks for Hawaii and she was going back to Detroit. It added a sense of urgency to the situation. There was no possibility of a long-term relationship. There was just a hot, passionate fling. It lasted for about a week and then she went back home. Shortly thereafter, I ended up in Hawaii. Ostensibly, I was taking some classes but in actuality, I was primarily surfing all of the classic breaks on the south shore and the north shore of the island. I really can't remember anything about the courses I took at the university but I do remember my passion for surfing. In all, I was on Oahu for eight months.

At first, I lived in Waikiki, but for the majority of my stay I lived on Kainui Road along with a pack of young surfers. In the morning, afternoon and evening, whenever the surf was up, we would step out of our door and bring our boards down the beach to the Bonsai Pipeline.

December came and the weather grew stormy thousands of miles away at sea which produced huge swells and prodigious surf. On Christmas day we all piled into a Volkswagen van and went to Waimea Bay. We stood for hours watching the giant waves crest and crash on the shore. Finally three surfers, two experts and a novice, paddled out to attempt to ride the 30-foot walls of water. The experts were guys who had braved the elements and surfed the big ones for years. The novice was a lanky 21-year-old, me.

I managed to stay on my board and I didn't die, I am happy to say. At the end of the day there were plenty of people to pat me on the back and loads of girls in bikinis who were suitably impressed.

One of the side benefits of surfing, aside from the exercise, was the girls. It was amazing how many beautiful girls were in Hawaii. There was only one problem. I was in love with Detroit Sharon. I wrote to her almost every day. In truth, I was a shy young man and afraid of dating and somewhat socially inept. It was a very convenient way of avoiding my shy nature when relating to girls. I was in a relationship, at least in my mind, so I thought that going out with other women would be a betrayal.

I did have a few dates while I was on the North Shore. I didn't avoid all of the many opportunities presenting themselves to me. But, if I went out for a beer with a girl, there would actually be three of us sitting at the table – me, my date and the ghost of Sharon. I was never fully present with any date because I was somehow comparing her to the growing list of attributes I had assigned to Detroit Sharon in my ever-expanding fantasy about who she was and what she meant to me.

This long distance relationship served many purposes. I could consider myself in a relationship, so I never actually had to confront my fear of dating and the possibility of being rejected. The fantasy of Detroit Sharon sustained me in my aloneness. I siphoned off the intensity of the moment with dreams of our time together from the past, which were now re-scripted to be larger than life while constructing a happily-ever-after scenario for the future.

You would think that as a surfer I was interested in experiencing the intensity of life. Perhaps so, but interpersonally I was inept and insecure. During those eight months, even though I was 21 and single and relatively available, I only dated two or three ladies. Those dates never really amounted to anything since my heart was attached to my fantasy relationship with Detroit Sharon.

As the time grew closer to leaving Hawaii, I arranged my flight home via Detroit. What I found was not the long anticipated reunion, but rather a rude awakening. The shocking truth was that it took me all of one day to realize the "mistake" I had made. Sharon was still cute but we had nothing in common and it didn't take long to see that I didn't even really like her. Suddenly, I realized that the person I had fantasized about was just that, a fantasy. This person only looked like the Sharon of my dreams. The two of us limped through the rest of our visit and it was with mutual relief when I took my leave. Sharon eventually went on to become a lawyer and a judge and I went on to New York and the rest of my life.

Nowadays, when people tell us about their long distance relationships, I am reminded of those eight months I spent in Hawaii rejecting many beautiful women for the fantasy of my "relationship." I had thought that something or someone in the future, namely Sharon, was going to save me. But then, when I got back to New York, I kept complaining to myself about having missed all of those beautiful, bikini-clad girls. My life at that time was a pendulum swing between the past and the future and Detroit Sharon had acted as a very convenient shield between me and living my life.

It is easy to be seduced by the dream of a better "someday" or the fantasy of how the past was so fine. These flights of fancy are convenient side trips when faced with something new or challenging that has yet to be mastered. From time-to-time I chuckle when I think of Detroit Sharon and the lesson I learned about not throwing away this moment for some fictitious "someday" that, in fact, will never come.

THE MAJESTY OF THE MOMENT
As told by Ariel

In early September 2004, our first day offshore in Venezuela, Shya caught and released his very first white marlin using a fly rod. Photo ops abounded at this exciting acrobatic, dancing, leaping event.

Earlier that day, the ocean was calm, calm, calm. Very unusual for that particular place, so we were told. But as we came into port at the end of our offshore adventure, we found out that the marina would be closed the following day. They were anticipating hurricane Ivan (the terrible), which was predicted to come closer to Venezuela than any hurricane ever had.

Due to where the country is located, big cyclones usually scoot by and leave the coastline unmolested. Although the storm was happening to the east and north of us, there was the expectation of big swells rolling in from the sea. On a walk around the marina, we found that the general consensus among the staff and crews of the docked boats was that closing the marina was a colossal over-reaction. Chances were, they said, that this would be another beautiful day.

After a meal of fresh fish and a glass of wine we retired, not knowing what to expect in the morning. We awoke in the middle of the night to the sound of rain pounding on the roof, the deluge of a tropical storm.

By morning the rain had stopped, but when we stepped out of our door and strolled to the boats, we could feel the adrenaline. People there were still rocking and reeling from the trauma of December 1999, when after 16 days of nonstop rain, the mountains along 65 miles of coast let loose. Tons of mud, rocks and debris had fallen into the sea just after midnight when most people were in bed. There were workers at the marina who had their entire village destroyed. One young man reportedly helped pull 50 people from the mud and destruction, saving their lives. His home was only one of four buildings left standing in his village after the slide. So with the prediction of extreme weather, the villagers who had survived that tragedy were on edge.

As we walked out along the dock we could feel the tension. Thirty million dollars worth of boats were lined up at the marina, cheek-by-jowl, and crews were rushing to add extra lines and bumpers... all hands on deck kind of thing.

Soon the tide began to surge and the boats went "clackety-clack" all in a line from left to right as the water rushed into the marina. In the distance, we could see the surge begin to jump over the sea wall. Shya and I fortified ourselves with double espressos (we still have our priorities straight, hurricane or not) and then I retrieved my camera and began snapping shots of the preparations. When some of the local men saw me, camera in hand, they suggested we climb to the roof of a nearby half-completed building (construction stopped after the mudslide of '99 and had not yet resumed) if we wanted an unobstructed, bird's eye view. We followed them through the dark and dusty underground garage, past the detritus of big boats, banged up props and the like, and began the assent to the roof. It was kind of eerie up there with half-finished railings and an open elevator shaft.

As we climbed the stairs, we stepped over the imprint of an iguana. It had died right there and was absorbed as it decayed, until only a ghostly shadow was left. When we reached the top, we went to the penthouse windows, a breathless eleven floors up. We could still feel the controlled chaos as we watched those below us.

A 63-foot Garlington, a big blue-hulled beauty, motored further into the marina and farther from the mouth of the harbor. The surge had been so unexpectedly large and fierce, the stress had destroyed the cement cleats on the dock to which it had been tied. Now they needed to find a new place to safely moor their boat. We paid special attention to that boat's security, not only for them but also for us. This was the boat we had rented and all of our equipment was still onboard.

I began to take pictures as the sea first crested the seawall and then later as it went crashing in great massive waves. The seawall stood twenty feet but the swells were twenty-seven. Mountains of spray jetted skyward. The sailboats bobbed like toys. We could see brave souls clinging to masts with arms and legs, attempting to ride the storm. Soon the wind came up, sending sails lashing and flags whipping. And then, then the waves peaked and the worst had passed. Surprisingly, there was no rain. All was soon quiet.

The next morning, we found out that three people at the outer marina died that day. Hungry waves had devoured the docks and boats and men. Five surfers who foolishly had attempted to ride the walls of water also had perished, but our boat had weathered the storm without so much as a scratch. Later, as we rode past the destruction and out to sea, I found myself thinking about those lost souls.

I doubt that they woke up in the morning and knew it would be their last day on earth. They probably had plans for the next day and for the weekend ahead and for their lives. I found myself saying silent prayers for the victims and the grieving families of the men. It was one of those instances where I had a direct experience of the impermanence of things. One where I was grateful for the quirk of fate that left the two of us safe to live another day. There was still time for our lives to continue to unfold.

Shya and I had been brushed by the wingtips of nature's fury, a single feather touch that left us trembling. It was a reminder of the preciousness and fragility of life and also of the majesty of the moment.

ACKNOWLEDGMENTS

We are thankful to Paul English, who started us on the journey of expressing our reality in written form – this book would not be without you.

We deeply appreciate those in our transformational community. You are a true source of inspiration. We appreciate your partnership in sharing enlightenment with others. The world needs more people like you.

Specifically we thank those who so selflessly gave of their time and energy on this manuscript... in all its iterations. You are a blessing.

ABOUT THE KANES

Ariel and Shya Kane are internationally acclaimed authors, seminar leaders and consultants whose transformational approach allows people to discover satisfaction and increased productivity in all areas of their lives, without working on their "problems." They are expert guides who, with great skill and humor, bring people through the swamp of the mind into the clarity and brilliance of the moment.

Acting as Catalysts for Personal Transformation, the Kanes provide ongoing consulting and seminars for a range of clients from individuals and couples to entrepreneurs and Fortune 500 companies. In their seminar programs, they have created an environment in which thousands have experienced dramatic improvements in the quality of their lives.

FOR FURTHER INFORMATION

Visit the Kanes' website **www.ask-inc.com** to find out more about seminars, audios and books, and to sign up to receive their online newsletter, article of the month and podcasts.